CRAFTSMEN

SKILLFULLY LEADING YOUR FAMILY FOR CHRIST

JOHN CROTTS

Shepherd Press
Wapwallopen, Pennsylvania

Craftsmen

© 2005 by John Crotts

ISBN 0-9767582-3-7

Unless otherwise noted, Scripture quotations are from The Holy Bible, English Standard Version (ESV), Copyright © 2001 by Crossway Bibles, a division of Good News Publishers.

Italics or bold text within Scripture quotations indicate emphasis added.

Page design and typesetting by Lakeside Design Plus

Printed in the United States of America

CRAFTSMEN

To Lynn
You are a precious gift from the Lord to me.
He has used you to help and encourage me in every way.
Thank you for your wise example and input.

TABLE OF CONTENTS

ACKNOWLEDGEMENTS

THE PATH TO CRAFTSMANSHIP is no lonely road. As the Lord uses many means of making us into the people he desires, he has also used many people to bring this book to completion.

Thanks to Rick Irvin and the team at Shepherd Press for their willingness to take on this project and make it better with their thoughtful input.

It has been my delight to serve as the pastor of Faith Bible Church of Sharpsburg, Georgia since 1995. Getting to serve the Lord by shepherding his people alongside dear elders and friends has been a wonderful privilege. They are a constant encouragement in the ways they hear and apply God's Word. Truly, the Lord has used them to help me grow in wisdom as much or more than I have been used to help them.

Anna Maupin has been a great friend through the editing process. Her red pen sacrificed much ink to make this book better in countless ways. My wife and I appreciate her and her husband Tony deeply.

Special thanks to Bill May for his great help with the discussion questions. As a gifted teacher, Bill has a knack for taking challenging subjects and personalizing the application with sharp questions.

I was blessed to grow up in a Christian home in Virginia. My parents, John and Jane Crotts, instilled many lessons of skillful living from my youth up. My brother Jeff, who is a pastor in Little Rock, and his wife Judy and their kids Riley, Logan, and Emmie have also proven to be wonderful sources of godly wisdom to our family. Thank you all.

My precious wife Lynn and our daughters Charissa, Danielle, and Chloe are a continuous blessing to me. The Lord has used them to shape me and encourage me in every way. Virtually all of the lessons of this book have been forged and applied first from within the walls of our home.

Most of all, I must thank my Lord Jesus Christ. He has mercifully forgiven my foolishness. He has given me his wisdom, and is building his wisdom into me. It is only because of his grace that I have anything to pass on to my wife, children, church, and you.

INTRODUCTION

THE CRAFTSMAN CAN TAKE a stack of wood and produce a beautiful piece of furniture. He not only possesses intellectual abilities to follow a blueprint or step-by-step instructions, but he is also an artist. His hands manipulate the wood into beautiful shapes. His eyes anticipate the right cuts and movements. His workmanship causes others to wonder at his skill.

My friend, David Peace, is such a craftsman. David works full time as a firefighter and paramedic. On his off days he opened a custom cabinet shop. While I may have the ability to follow instructions and get by with the results, in a short time, with no formal training, David has built exquisite cabinetry and fixtures for half-a-million dollar homes. Most recently, our church hired David to oversee the construction of our entire church building. God has blessed David with the unusual skill and ability to work with wood. The results have been impressive.

Such craftsmanship has an application for all men. While I may never be able to create the products of a master cabinet maker, I am responsible to create my life with equal skill.

Every area of my life as a Christian man must be molded by the wisdom of God. My words, my work, my relationships, and even the way I use my resources must flow from a heart gripped by the character of God. Such a heartbeat for God's glory will practically result in a life skillfully lived.

This book is designed to simplify the quest for wisdom. The first section, The Foundation, will seek to unlock the meaning of wisdom and its basis—the fear of God. We will also see how the Lord Jesus Christ is the ultimate Wise Man. The second section, The Handiwork, will apply God's wisdom to various areas of leadership and living. While the book of Proverbs will be the starting point for our studies, attention will be given to the rest of Scripture as well. Our goal should not be to help ourselves with mere practical pointers. Real life change only occurs as we see the Lord Jesus Christ and seek to conform our lives to his by the power of the Holy Spirit.

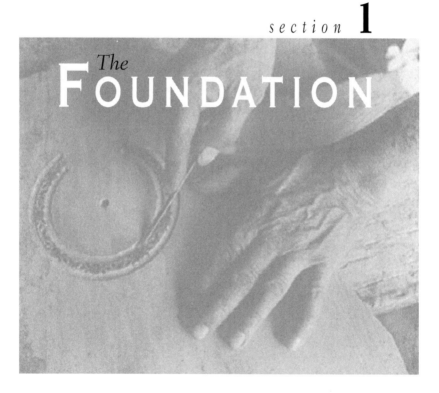

section 1

The
FOUNDATION

1

THE MEANING OF WISDOM

DON'T WE ALL HAVE THE SAME PICTURE of the Wise Man in our minds? He is very old. He is bald with leathery skin and a very long white beard. For some reason, he is short and stubby. He wears a robe or tunic of some kind and sometimes carries an oversized book. He sits under a large shady tree on top of a mountain. The occasional searcher for wisdom, deep in thought about the mysteries of life, makes the fearsome climb to seek out the Ancient One. After the seeker catches his breath, he asks the question of his heart. The answer from this great guru, of course, makes no sense at all. But we figure since he is the wise one, and the searcher spent so much effort getting up the hill, it would make sense if only we were as enlightened as the master.

Though this comical picture of true wisdom is common, it is absolutely wrong. The Bible says nothing about this kind of wisdom. Rather than being vague and "out there", God's wisdom is completely practical. In fact, if you have been blessed with an oversized brain and an IQ that would make Einstein jealous, but you live as though God doesn't matter, you are just a big-headed fool. God's wisdom starts with an attitude (not an IQ) and then works out into a lifestyle. Understanding the meaning of wisdom is a foundational component of knowing what God wants us to strive for. As one wise man observed, "If you aim at nothing, you'll hit it every time!"

CONCEPT

The Hebrew word for wisdom is *hakam*. The basic meanings of this term are wise, skillful, or practical. The idea of *skillfulness* emerges from the way the term *hakam* is used in the Bible. For example, the Lord, through Moses, commissioned *skillful* people to make the garments of Aaron the high priest. "And you shall make holy garments for Aaron your brother, for glory and for beauty. You shall speak to all the skillful, whom I have filled with the spirit of skill, that they may make Aaron's garments to consecrate him for my priesthood" (Exodus 28:2–3). God actually endowed these people with *a spirit of wisdom* for the task. Being wise in this context has nothing to do with sitting under a tree meditating about the meaning of life. These men were skillful artists whirling needles and threads to produce a stunning garment for the man who would represent the people of God before him.

Another example of the word most often translated *wisdom* is found in Exodus 35:30–35. God calls men by name to be custom builders of God's tabernacle—Bezalel, and later Oholiab, along with others. These men were filled with "the Spirit of God, with skill, with intelligence, with knowledge, and with all craftsman-ship." God said he had "filled them with skill to do every sort of work done by an engraver or by a designer or by an embroiderer in blue and purple and scarlet yarns and fine twined linen, or by a weaver—by any sort of workman or skilled designer." Clearly, God only wanted the finest work done on his meeting place, and he empowered these men to do it.

While in some places in the Bible *hakam* means skillful like a craftsman, the meaning of the term wisdom in Proverbs implies more than skill with needles and thread, or hammers and chisels. Wisdom in Proverbs can be more narrowly defined as *mastering the art of skillful living*. As Richard Mayhue puts it in his book *Practicing Proverbs*, "Proverbs instructs about skillfully manifesting God's character and will in one's everyday life, making godly decisions, and being so oriented to God that one's life choices always please Him."[1] Wisdom involves learning God's ways from his Word, and then making right choices based upon his truth. Our consistency in making these right choices is an indication of our maturity and development in wisdom.[2]

CONNECTION

The practical meaning of wisdom in Proverbs is also uncovered by the connection between wisdom and right behavior. God's benchmark for evaluating a man's wisdom is directly related to how morally upright his lifestyle is. This connection jumps out of every chapter in the book of Proverbs. Notice the tremendous impact wisdom makes on a person's lifestyle in Proverbs 2:7–22. Nearly every line of this section about *wisdom* has something to say about *morality*.

> He stores up sound wisdom for the **upright**;
> he is a shield to those who **walk in integrity**,
> guarding the paths of **justice**
> and watching over the way of his saints.
> Then you will understand **righteousness and justice
> and equity, every good path**;

for wisdom will come into your heart,
and knowledge will be pleasant to your soul;
discretion will watch over you,
understanding will guard you,
delivering you from the **way of evil**,
from men of **perverted speech**,
who forsake the **paths of uprightness**
to walk in the **ways of darkness**,
who rejoice in **doing evil**
and delight in the **perverseness of evil**,
men whose **paths are crooked**,
and who are **devious** in their ways.
So you will be delivered from the **forbidden woman**,
from the adulteress with her **smooth words**,
who **forsakes the companion of her youth**
and **forgets the covenant of her God**;
for her house sinks down to death,
and her paths to the departed;
none who go to her come back,
nor do they regain the paths of life.
So you will walk in the **way of the good**
and keep to the **paths of the righteous**.
For the **upright** will inhabit the land,
and those with **integrity** will remain in it,
but the **wicked** will be cut off from the land,
and the **treacherous** will be rooted out of it.

(emphasis added)

You may think you are wise, but does your lifestyle match up with what God desires? Are you upright, blameless, righteous, and just? Are you a man of integrity and sexual purity? Do you hate pride, perverted speech, and evil? If there is a mismatch between your morality and your claims of wisdom, then use your lifestyle as the final judge of your level of wisdom.

If you are to be a skillful leader of your family, this responsibility will always start with your lifestyle. To grow in leadership means growing in a godly lifestyle. To grow in godliness means growing in God's wisdom.

CLOSE PARALLELS

In the introduction to the book of Proverbs, Solomon flanks the word wisdom with several parallel words. This array of descriptive words should not be understood as referring to different concepts, however, because the terms expand, reinforce, and enrich the meaning of the concept of wisdom.[3]

> The proverbs of Solomon, son of David, king of Israel:
> To know **wisdom** and **instruction**,
> to **understand** words of **insight**,
> to receive instruction in wise dealing,
> in righteousness, justice, and equity;
> to give **prudence** to the simple,
> **knowledge** and **discretion** to the youth—
> Let the wise hear and increase in **learning**,
> and the one who understands obtain **guidance**,
> to understand a proverb and a saying,
> the words of the wise and their riddles.
> (Proverbs 1:1–6, emphasis added)

Old Testament scholar Derek Kidner describes these parallel terms to wisdom as "breaking up the plain daylight of wisdom into its rainbow of constituent colors." He goes on to say, "These all shade into one another, and any one of them can be used to represent the whole; yet there is . . . value in seeing them momentarily analyzed and grouped."[4] Let's follow Kidner's suggestion and consider each of these parts to better grasp wisdom's whole meaning.

Instruction includes the ideas of correction and discipline. It is frequently a companion of the word reproof.[5] Shepherding children

19

requires more than just sitting back spouting off proper facts about behavior. Even in teaching Charissa, my oldest daughter, to play softball, I can't pontificate. I have to repeat the lesson again and again. I often have to include correction with my instruction to get the wisdom to take hold. "Don't hold the glove down when the ground ball is coming above your waist, it could pop out and hit you in the face." "That's right, hold your glove facing up to field the ball and make the play."

Understanding involves looking at the heart of an issue and discerning the differences at stake in the choices being weighed.[6] A wise person of understanding can read between the lines to be able to make the best possible choice.[7]

In 1 Samuel 25, Abigail demonstrates this kind of understanding. Although David and his men had faithfully provided protection for her husband Nabal's shepherds and flocks, allowing Nabal to grow wealthy, Nabal stubbornly refused David's request for provisions. David and his men strapped on their swords to extract their due supplies, but Abigail quickly assessed the situation and went into action.

As David angrily approached, Abigail went to meet him with two hundred loaves of bread, two jugs of wine, five prepared sheep, five measures of roasted grain, a hundred clusters of raisins, and two hundred cakes of figs (1 Samuel 25:18). Before David could even get to Nabal's home, though, Abigail bowed before Israel's future king, took full responsibility for Nabal's offense, gave David the gracious gift she had prepared, and blessed him in the Lord's name. David's anger was completely pacified through Abigail's wise actions. Within a week and a half the Lord struck Nabal dead. When David heard this, he sent a wedding proposal to make this woman of understanding his wife.

Prudence can mean shrewdness, cunning, cleverness, or even deceit.[8] In the context of godly wisdom, prudence means shrewdness or cleverness in the best senses of the terms. Proverbs 1:3, seen above, speaks of prudence as wise dealing, righteousness, justice, and equity.

To demonstrate the tremendous wisdom of Solomon, 1 Kings 3:16–28 relates the account of two prostitutes with infants coming to the king for a judgment. One of the women has accidentally killed her son by rolling onto him during the night. Before the other wakes up, though, the mother of the dead child secretly switches the babies. Of course the mother of the live baby knows what had happened and demands to have her baby back. They go before Solomon to resolve the matter. The shrewd king, Solomon, declares that the living child should be chopped in two so that each woman could receive half. Horrified, the true mother would rather lose the baby than have her son cut in two. When she offers the whole child to the false mother, Solomon knows she is the true mother and awards the baby to her. After the nation heard about this verdict, they were amazed at the prudence that God had bestowed on their king.

Knowledge in Proverbs is not merely knowing information; it is knowing and doing what God requires as consistently as possible.[9] The word for knowledge is used as a direct parallel with *wisdom* in verses describing the fear of the Lord (Proverbs 1:7; 9:10). Like wisdom, the idea of knowledge in these passages is not *knowing* facts, but putting them into practice skillfully.

It is a sad truth that many people have vast head knowledge about the facts of the Bible without any real life application. Certain professors, pastors, and even authors of Bible commentaries have made entire careers out of studying the Bible without believing one word of the book they have so thoroughly dissected.

Discretion focuses upon prudent planning.[10] While there are many examples of careful planning, Solomon selected one from among God's smallest creatures in order to instruct his son. He observed that the ant, even though she is small, not very strong, and lacks a tough task-master, "prepares her bread in summer and gathers her food in harvest" (Proverbs 6:8). We will examine the ant's example of wise hard work later, but for now notice her discretion in planning ahead for the cold winter. My wife and I have some friends who carefully plan their meals for the entire month, but ants literally plan their meals as much as half a year in advance.

Learning means to receive or grasp the truth.[11] Learning in relation to wisdom is comprehending the truth of God well enough to pass it on to someone else.[12] An expression used by preachers is, "A mist in the pulpit means a fog in the pew." When a pastor fails to understand the point of a passage of Scripture it is pretty certain that his listeners will have no idea what's going on. In the same way, you will never be able to instruct others in wisdom (or lead them!) by word or example, until you have a personal comprehension of God's wisdom.

Guidance is wise counsel or accurate leadership.[13] Imagine a ship in heavy fog, trapped in a dangerous storm. The captain is seeking to navigate the difficulties using various instruments, consulting his officers, crying out for help over the radio, and perhaps straining to spy the beam of the lighthouse. The more sure and steady the counsel he receives, the more help he has in facing his greatest challenge. In the same way, wise counsel helps us navigate through life.

CONTRAST

The variety of terms used in the Proverbs to describe wisdom help us to grasp its meaning. Another way to understand a concept, however, is by examining its opposite. You can teach someone to appreciate the sharp angles of a square not only by pointing out positive examples of the squares themselves, but also by contrasting squares with circles. Likewise, the Proverbs do not merely sing the virtues of wisdom, they also offer pointed descriptions of foolishness.

The Fool

> The fear of the LORD is the beginning of knowledge;
> fools despise wisdom and instruction.
> (Proverbs 1:7)

> Doing wrong is like a joke to a fool,
> but wisdom is pleasure to a man of understanding.
> (Proverbs 10:23)

> The fool says in his heart, "There is no God."
> They are corrupt, they do abominable deeds,
> there is none who does good.
> (Psalm 14:1)

Throughout the Bible, the character most unlike the wise person is the fool. Like the variety of parallel words for wisdom, Proverbs uses several different terms for the concept of foolishness.

The key Hebrew words which are translated as *fool* ('ewil, and nebalah), add up to the same meaning. A fool is someone who lacks wisdom, even despising it. He also despises the discipline necessary to attain wisdom. So maybe we could say a *golf fool* would be someone who not only hits every ball into the woods, but also hates hearing about how he could improve his game. He refuses to practice, and becomes obstinate even when Tiger Woods drops by to offer a few tips. Mental equipment is not the issue in foolishness. Being a fool is a chosen lifestyle. The fool has a character that is selfish, stubborn, and pigheaded. He declares, "My way or the highway!" He lives as if God does not exist instead of living reverently in light of the reality of God.

23

The Fool's Gallery

In addition to the terms translated *fool*, considering two other characters in the fool's gallery in Proverbs helps us understand the concept of foolishness.

The **Scoffer** moves beyond the fool's random mischief to the deliberate damage of ridicule and disparagement.[14] This person is not content to wallow in his own personal mud hole of foolishness, he actively uses his mouth to spread his sin to others. The Lord Jesus Christ said there is a direct pipeline between a person's heart and a person's mouth. "For out of the abundance of the heart the mouth speaks" (Matthew 12:34). A scoffer is a person with a heart of refined foolishness. Because of the folly fully developed in this person's heart, a cynical tongue is inevitable.

The **Sluggard** is a close relative of Mr. Scoffer. He is lazy and selfish. He will not plan ahead. He will not work. He will not save money. He begins to believe his own excuses for his laziness.[15] While the ant tirelessly toils, storing up provisions for the winter, Mr. Sluggard watches from under a shade tree. Day after day the ant thoughtfully prepares for the future. Day after day Mr. Sluggard wastes time indulging his desires for pleasure, while constantly excusing himself from work. He lives for the now, so when the dark days of the future come, he is desperately trying to survive. Fools live short lives for obvious reasons.

The Naïve

Another character found in Proverbs is the naïve or simple person. While in some ways he is related to the fool, in other ways he is not quite as hopeless. The Hebrew word for "simple" means to be gullible, easily lead, or morally irresponsible.[16]

The simple believes everything,
but the prudent gives thought to his steps.
(Proverbs 14:15)

While adults can be naive, teenagers provide a prime example of the meaning of the word. Teenagers are beginning to move from dependence upon their parents towards increasing independence. They take on greater responsibilities and receive more privileges. Often, though, trouble comes into their lives due to their inexperience. The temptations of the world create challenging situations for the untried young man or woman. They can easily become spiritually sidetracked by making wrong choices in response to new temptations because of their naiveté.

The prudent sees danger and hides himself,
but the simple go on and suffer for it.
(Proverbs 22:3)

Many teens are taken in by bad deals. Unfaithful friends sting them. They are seduced sexually. Many children are conceived in the wombs of naive young ladies. The naive are in a dangerous stage of life.

Naiveté is not restricted to young men. How many men naively let their children surf the internet unsupervised? How many Dads don't stop their daughters from leaving the house dressed to seduce? How many men watch all kinds of sleaze on TV with their kids? Do you know the character of your kids' friends? There are appalling consequences waiting just ahead for simple men.

The Proverbs give the most sober warning a naive man could hear—you can graduate to become a fool.

The simple inherit folly,
but the prudent are crowned with knowledge.
(Proverbs 14:18)

According to Derek Kidner, "One does not stay still; a man who is empty headed will end up wrong headed."[17] The classic example of the naive man is found in Proverbs 7:6–23. Solomon tells the story of an aimless, inexperienced man drifting along, dangerously dancing with temptation. Instead of carefully avoiding a tempting situation, this young man passes along the streets where the adulterous woman lurks. Certainly, Solomon paints this woman with guilty words of seductive dress and flattering and persistent words of temptation. The young man's naiveté is seen as he puts himself in harm's way, listens to her seductive words, and finally goes along with her. Solomon also highlights his ignorance of the consequences of his actions. "All at once he follows her, as an ox goes to the slaughter, or as a stag is caught fast till an arrow pierces its liver; as a bird rushes into a snare; he does not know that it will cost him his life" (Proverbs 7:22–23).

The young simple man is interested in trying something new and exciting. He likes the element of risk and sneaking around at night. A sexy woman is interested in him! The most dangerous quality of a naive person is he thinks he can handle temptations. He underestimates the seductive power of sin, and is ignorant of sin's deadly consequences. Solomon's simple man became enticed; he sinned; and he ultimately dies. The naive man has now had his graduation ceremony. He is now a fool, and will suffer the consequences of being a fool.

A naive person is not yet as guilty or as hopeless as a full-fledged fool, but he is well on his way. The naive person could be called an F.I.T.—a Fool-In-Training. We could create a chart to help us track his path.

Scoffing Fool	Naïve	Wise Man
1	5	10

Where are you on this chart? In which direction are you moving? Remember, you are *never* standing still. If you think you are, you are surely moving backwards. There are rich rewards for wisdom and serious consequences for foolishness. You now know the stark dangers of being naive. Are you continuing to coast along the Fool's Highway? This is very serious—life and death are ultimately on the line. Even your eternal destination is at stake. While you might not suffer the fruit of your folly today or tomorrow, be certain that your foolishness will always catch you.

True wisdom is more than just sitting under a tree and philosophizing about life. It involves the hard work of craftsmanship. The wise craftsman searches out inspired truth from the Book of God and then carefully seeks to apply those truths to real-life situations. The result of this lifestyle craftsmanship is not about a bald head, beard, and a permanent spot on a high hill for people to come to seek out your wisdom, but a life that others recognize as skillfully lived. A wise life is a life worth living and a life worth following.

Study Questions—CHAPTER 1

1. According to the definition of God's wisdom, compare the role of a person's attitude to that of his IQ.
2. Three terms that help describe the meaning of the Hebrew word for wisdom are:

_____

_____

_____

3. In Proverbs, wisdom is portrayed as mastering the art of skillful living. Describe the two main components that are necessary for skillful living.
4. What is a reliable indicator regarding your maturity and development in wisdom?
5. Describe examples of the relationship between wisdom and right behavior as they are portrayed in Proverbs.
6. Explain the significance of God's benchmark of a man's wisdom based on each individual lifestyle. How would you judge your own personal level of wisdom?
7. What is the impact on a man's life when he grows in godliness?
8. List seven components of being wise that will help you to grasp the concept of wisdom.
9. When describing a person who is unwise, the Bible refers to this character as a _____.
10. In Proverbs we can see examples of the type of person considered as being unwise. Three characters that are described as fools are _____, _____, and the _____. Give a brief description that identifies the characteristics of each of the above examples.

GUT CHECK:

Based on the chart on page 26, place an "X" where you see yourself in regards to being a wise man.

- In what direction are you headed? Remember there is no such thing as sitting still.
- What is your plan of action in your quest for wisdom?

2

THE BEGINNING
OF WISDOM

THE TIGER EXHIBIT AT ZOO ATLANTA is one of my favorites.
Behind a great glass barrier is a green hill filled with all sorts
of plants and trees. The tigers always seem to be lying at the
highest corner of the exhibit, though, often making them
difficult to see. But if you look hard you can see the beautiful, sleek, and powerful cat looking back at you. Suppose,
because the tigers hide in the remotest part of their habitat,
some senseless family decided to have their picnic lunch on
this beautiful hillside?

Perhaps for some time they will enjoy their sandwiches,
fresh fruits, and potato chips on a warm Atlanta day—even
with frantic spectators on the right side of the thick glass
trying to get their attention. This foolish family is eating and
relaxing as if the tiger in the corner does not exist because
they don't see him. Even though they are happily ignoring the

tiger, it doesn't mean that he is ignoring them. This tiger's going to be having a picnic of his own at any moment!

While hopefully no one is so foolish as to really try to have a picnic with the tigers (and the zoo goes to great lengths to prevent anyone who does have such crazy ideas), many men foolishly walk through life as if *God* does not exist. The Bible calls this the fundamental mark of a fool.

> The fool says in his heart, "There is no God."
> They are corrupt, they do abominable deeds,
> there is none who does good.
> (Psalm 14:1)

Without any thought that God is watching their every movement, listening to their words, and even inspecting the motivations of their hearts, a countless number of men live without the slightest thought of God. Even if they give lip service to his existence and deep down suppose he exists in a corner somewhere, these guys go about their routines without the slightest concern for what God thinks or what He may do to them. As foolish as the family having lunch with the tiger would be, living as if the God of the Bible does not exist or does not matter is *infinitely more foolish*. After all, all the tiger can do is rip you to shreds and eat you for lunch. God, on the other hand, can and will send to hell all those who spurn him.

WHERE WISDOM BEGINS

True wisdom begins by living according to the *reality* that the God of the Bible does exist and cares very much about our lifestyle. What may seem like an old-fashioned concept is actually *the* foundation of a life that pleases the Lord. It's Reality 101. Proverbs 9:10 tells us, "The fear of God is the beginning of wisdom." The fear of the Lord is the very first step onto the Path of Wisdom. The basic definition of the fear of the Lord is "reverential awe." While this definition is correct, according to Jerry Bridges, it is open to misunderstanding because today we use the words "awe" or "awesome" in such casual ways.[1] We call God awesome, but we also call chocolate sundaes awesome.

The proper definition of the word awe is "an emotion in which dread, veneration, and wonder are variously mingled." This definition certainly applies to a right view of Almighty God, and this certainly *does not* apply to ice cream (no matter how good)![2]

The Components of the Fear of God

In order to pull together what we have learned about this great first step down the Way of Wisdom, let's consider three fundamental components of the fear of God. These are the basic building blocks of reverence for the Lord.

Component 1: A Realization of Who God Is

The more you know about the character of God that is revealed to us in the Bible, the more reverence will fill your heart. Consider some of the attributes of God. The Bible teaches that God *created the heavens and the earth*. Far from being the accidental collision of random molecules, you and I and everything around us in nature are the direct result of God's handiwork.

The Bible also reveals that God is *perfectly just*. Almost everyone cringes at the thought that criminals sometime evade prison time because a clever lawyer sways a jury with an emotional victimization story. But ultimately, no one gets away with anything. Justice is not guaranteed because earthly judges are perfectly wise and just, but because God is. He never misses one shred of evidence, and his gavel always strikes with perfect precision. If you do not see justice here, rest assured it will be clear at the Judgment.

The Lord is also *holy*. Holiness means separation. God is completely separate from and over all of his creation. God is also completely separate from all forms of evil. Sin will not be tolerated in his presence. When Isaiah saw the vision of the Lord seated in the temple in Isaiah 6:3, one mighty angel cried out to another,

> "Holy, holy, holy is the LORD of hosts;
> the whole earth is full of his glory!"

The Scriptures also reveal that God *knows everything* that is, that was, and that will be. He is *all-powerful*. He is *all-wise*. He is *everywhere-present*. He is a God of wrath, and a God of glory. The fear of God really begins to develop when you realize that you truly will stand before this holy and righteous judge and give an account of *every one of your words and deeds*.

There are at least three other attributes of God that make the profound difference between a Christian version of the fear of God and a non-Christian's version. If a non-Christian were to get a true understanding of God's hatred for sin and the certain judgment to come, he would live in sheer *terror* of God. Even Adam and Eve in the Garden of Eden, after their fall into sin, hid from the presence of God out of fear.[3] A Christian, however, has seen more of God's character than his justice and wrath. He has also seen God's love, mercy, and grace. The combination of all of God's attributes is most powerfully displayed at the cross of Jesus. At the death of Jesus, God's righteous wrath against sin *and* his love, mercy, and grace for sinners came together, as Jesus bore the wrath of God on behalf of God's children.[4]

Far from being a sharp contradiction, a God to be feared and a God who loves us harmonizes beautifully. An appreciation of God's grace *in spite* of our many sins melts our *terror* of the Lord into *awe* for One so holy and just, while at the same time so kind and merciful. This truth is seen in both the Old and the New Testaments.

> If you, O LORD, should mark iniquities,
>   O Lord, who could stand?
> But with you there is forgiveness,
>   that you may be feared.
>   (Psalm 130:3–4)

Or do you presume on the riches of his kindness and forbearance and patience, not knowing that God's kindness is meant to lead you to repentance?

(Romans 2:4)

Professor Sinclair Ferguson wisely observed, "One reason why we know so little of such filial [child-like] fear is that we do not appreciate the gospel."[5] Appreciating the gospel means tasting the bitterness of our deep sinfulness, realizing the eternal wrath justly due us, and seeing by faith the Lord Jesus Christ bearing the sum total of that wrath in our place on the cross. Even the present-day sins of mature Christians find their forgiveness back upon Jesus' cross. The sins we commit today, in spite of our great Bible knowledge and experience of God's ongoing grace, are much more serious than those committed when we barely knew better. Yet, even these terrible sins were overpowered by the grace of God because of Jesus' bloody death on the cross.

The first component of the fear of God is to realize who God really is. The second step actually is drawn from one of the attributes we have just seen in considering God's character.

Component 2: **A Realization of Where God Is and What He Knows**

The attribute often called omnipresence recognizes that God is everywhere. The personal implication for us is that He is ALWAYS where you are. Related to God's omnipresence is his omniscience, which means God knows everything. Therefore, this holy, just, loving, and merciful God we have just learned about knows and sees EVERYTHING we *say*, and *do*, and *think*. He even knows the very motivations that lead to our actions (1 Corinthians 4:4–5).

Why is pornography on the internet such a stumbling block for men? It seems like no one is watching. It seems like all of the free lust you can stand, in the privacy of your own dark room. What a business traveler would never consider clicking on in the hotel lobby is fair game up in his locked room. Why are men ashamed to be seen by strangers in a hotel glancing at what they are not ashamed to be gazing on in the presence of God alone? Every sin you have committed in the darkness or under cover behind closed doors was actually just as plain and visible to God as if you had done it before his very throne, naked, with spot lights glaring down upon you.

Wise King Solomon used this truth to motivate his son to avoid committing adultery.

> For a man's ways are before the eyes of the Lord,
> and he ponders all his paths.
> (Proverbs 5:21)

Other places in Proverbs also remind us of the omnipresence and omniscience of God.

> The eyes of the LORD are in every place,
> keeping watch on the evil and the good.
> (Proverbs 15:3)

All the ways of a man are pure in his own eyes,
but the Lord weighs the spirit.

(Proverbs 16:2)

The author of Hebrews agrees that God knows us inside out.

For the word of God is living and active, sharper than any two-edged sword, piercing to the division of soul and of spirit, of joints and of marrow, and discerning the thoughts and intentions of the heart. And no creature is hidden from his sight, but all are naked and exposed to the eyes of him to whom we must give account.

(Hebrews 4:1–13)

A right understanding of God's character coupled with the thought of God's searching presence with you always leads you to live a radically different lifestyle. Knowing God's requirements is the third component in fearing the Lord.

Component 3: **A Realization of What God Demands of Us**

There is a connection between the fear of God and the Word of God. Not only does the Bible reveal God's character, thereby increasing our awe in his presence, but it also reveals God's will for men through his commandments. Whether you obey God or not is a big deal. Sound wisdom is not to take or leave at your leisure. The Great Creator demands that his creatures obey all of his commandments. Jesus said, "If you love me, you will keep my commandments" (John 14:15).

Disobeying God, even in the small stuff, is never trivial. When a God-fearing man gets too much change back in the store, he returns the excess, because God said, "You shall not steal!" (Exodus 20:15). A person who fears the Lord does not tell "white lies" to avoid hurting someone's feelings, because God said, "You shall not lie!" (Exodus 20:16). Because the Lord said, "Honor your father

37

and your mother" (Exodus 20:12), the wise person does not even backhandedly insult his mother. A God-fearer does not linger at magazine racks with lust-fueling covers prancing before his eyes. Why? Because Jesus said that entertaining lustful thoughts is committing adultery in your heart (Matthew 5:27–28). Remember, the God-fearer is also keenly aware that God is literally watching his eyes and heart in the magazine aisle of the store.

All three of these basic components of the fear of the Lord are true about God whether a person believes them or not. Just as the picnicking family's wrong beliefs about the tiger didn't change reality, neither do the wrong thoughts men think about God alter his existence. For example, if a man likes to think of God as only loving, that does not change the fact that the Bible says that God is angry at the wicked every day. If a guy thinks he is successfully hiding from God, he is dead wrong. There are no hiding places from God. And everyone will face God's judgment, whether they believe they will or not.[6]

The reason the fear of God is the absolute beginning of wisdom is because living in light of God's person, presence, and precepts is the only lifestyle that accurately conforms to reality. Fearing God is living life as it really is—not that we will ever fully know his character, appreciate his presence, or be conscious of all of his commands, but it is the only attitude that puts us on wisdom's path. Fools, living as if God does not exist, are living a lie. Fearing God is not some advanced stage of elite Christianity, it is Reality 101.

Study Questions—CHAPTER 2

1. According to Psalm 14:1, what is the fundamental mark of a fool?

2. True wisdom begins by living according to the reality that the God of the Bible does exist. What does Proverbs 9:10 say about this beginning?

3. How does the "fear of the Lord" differ between a Christian and a non-Christian?

4. The fear of God can be divided into three basic components:

   _____

   _____

   _____

5. List at least five of the attributes of God that would serve to increase your reverence for him.

6. What is the significance in your life of God's attributes of love, mercy, and grace?

7. If you believed that God knows and sees everything that we say, do, and think, how would it change your lifestyle?

8. Describe the connection between the fear of God and the Word of God.

9. How does the belief or non-belief of God's attributes affect the reality of who God is?

10. Why is living in light of God's person, presence, and precepts the only lifestyle that accurately conforms to reality?

GUT CHECK:

Imagine what it will be like on Judgment Day when you stand before God and give an account of every one of your words and deeds.

- How does the thought of standing before a holy and righteous judge affect your fear of God?
- Are there any areas in your lifestyle that need to change in preparation for that day?

3

THE END
OF WISDOM

MR. WISDOM

Each year there are all sorts of contests and magazines attempting to select the world's most beautiful men and women. The pageants parade lovely ladies dressed in a variety of fashions, and sometimes include interviews and performing talents as well. The magazines are filled with pictures of the most attractive celebrities of the year. As for the men, we merely flex our pumped-up muscles to music or just smile for the cameras.

If there were such a thing as a wisdom pageant, who would be this year's Mr. or Miss Wise? Would it be a man of keen business savvy like Microsoft's Bill Gates or Jack Welch, former head of GE? Perhaps some judges might nominate a religious figure like the Dalai Lama or the Pope. If the contest extended backward in history I'm sure that Martin Luther King, Jr. and Gandhi would be considered.

Those who know their Bible, though, would immediately think of King Solomon. When God appeared to him in a dream and asked what he wanted, Solomon requested wisdom. God made him the wisest man ever (see 1 Kings 3:3–14). But as wise as Solomon was, there came another who surpassed him—the Lord Jesus Christ. Where Solomon failed to live out the wisdom God had granted to him, Jesus perfectly succeeded.

God's wisdom isn't about brain power; it's about a heart filled with reverence for God that makes practical choices to do what God has revealed in his Word. The Bible closely connects wisdom with right behavior. Foolishness and sinfulness are simply two sides of the same coin. The critical implication for us is that whether we are wise or foolish is a very big deal to God. Although the Proverbs are filled with pictures of earthly rewards for wisdom and consequences for foolishness, the bigger reality is eternity. God sends fools to hell. Only the wise enter heaven.

While it is true that no man, apart from Jesus, has ever measured up to God's perfect standard of wisdom, God has not decided to grade on the curve. Just as his standard for holiness is his own perfection—"be holy for I am holy"—so also is his standard for practical wisdom his own perfection. While the goal of this book is to help you lead others as you lead yourself in God's wisdom, the fact is you'll never reach perfection. The good news is that Jesus Christ did live out perfect wisdom. And Jesus died for fools like you and me.

THE GREAT EXCHANGE

One verse in the New Testament offers the answer to this apparently impossible question of how someone who has acted foolishly can be declared right before an all-wise God. "He is the source of your life in Christ Jesus, whom *God made our wisdom* and our righteousness and sanctification and redemption" (1 Corinthians 1:30, emphasis added). The context in which this verse appears is about the cross of Christ. Although the world thinks the death of God's Son is a foolish concept, it is at the heart of God's wise message. Jesus Christ was so perfectly wise, he could die in the place of fools.

Second Corinthians 5:21 clearly spells out the concept of the substitution of Jesus in the place of sinners. "For our sake he made him to be sin who knew no sin, so that in him we might become the righteousness of God." God treated perfectly holy and wise Jesus as if he had committed our sins. He punished Jesus to death on the cross. He did this so that he could treat believers as if they had acted as perfectly righteous as Jesus had. This is the great exchange—our sinfulness for Jesus' righteousness. When we shine the light of 1 Corinthians 1:30 upon this exchange, we see that the exchange is also the trading of all our foolishness for all of Christ's wisdom. Those who humbly trust in the Lord Jesus Christ for their righteousness are also *declared wise* before God the Judge. While there is certainly an abundance of folly still lodged in your heart, the eternal record book reads "perfectly wise" on the basis of Jesus' work.

The practical importance of Jesus' wisdom is realizing that he is our source of wisdom and righteousness. Instead of pursuing wisdom and assuming we can earn God's favor or even excel on our own, our quest must flow *from the wisdom we have received in Jesus Christ*. Just as God regards us as righteous based on the righteousness of Jesus, so God regards us as wise based on the wisdom of Jesus. *On that basis* we must pursue practical wisdom. Because Jesus' wisdom is the basis of our own, let's take some time to consider the direct evidence of the wisdom of Jesus.[1]

THE WISDOM OF JESUS

Evidence 1: *The Visit from the Wise Men*

I live in the suburbs of Atlanta, Georgia, the home of an airport that always competes for the title of the world's busiest. The old joke is that even after a person dies, they have to change planes in Atlanta on the way to heaven. Suppose that somewhere in a remote Australian village a very special baby is born. When a group of Atlanta's finest pilots hear of his birth, they drop everything to journey thousands of treacherous miles to pay homage to this special boy. If these top pilots are willing to sacrifice such time and effort to honor the child, will not everyone who hears about him have astronomically high expectations for the potential pilot prodigy?

In a similar way, expectations about the wisdom of Jesus were ratcheted up in his childhood as the Magi, or Wise Men, from perhaps as far away as modern Iran, followed the star to pay homage to Jesus. Most likely their ancestors had been taught to expect the great Messiah from Daniel during his service in high posts in the Babylonian and the Media-Persian Empires.

When these men (most likely an entourage as opposed to just three) arrived in Jerusalem they began asking questions. "Where is he who has been born king of the Jews? For we saw his star when it rose and have come to worship him" (Matthew 2:2). When they found Jesus and his family in Bethlehem, they fell to the ground and worshipped him and gave him exquisite treasures of gold, frankincense, and myrrh (Matthew 2:11). While the Bible is filled with clearer direct examples of the wisdom of Jesus, Matthew does include this account for a reason. At least part of his purpose is to intensify his reader's expectations about the identity of this special child.

44

Evidence 2: *Jesus' Clear Growth in Wisdom*

In two places during the accounts of Jesus' early life on earth Luke offers summary statements to gather together the highlights of Jesus' growth to maturity. The first such statement occurs after Jesus' presentation in the temple when he is an infant. It summarizes the next twelve years of his life in Nazareth. "And when they had performed everything according to the Law of the Lord, they returned into Galilee, to their own town of Nazareth. And the child grew and became strong, **filled with wisdom**. And the favor of God was upon him" (Luke 2:39–40, emphasis added).

When Jesus was twelve, his parents brought him to Jerusalem for the Feast of the Passover. This was the time when he was accidentally left behind for three days. When finally discovered by his parents, Jesus is sitting among the religious scholars in the Temple amazing them with "his understanding and his answers" (Luke 2:47). After His parents find Him, Jesus returns with them to Nazareth.

In characterizing the years between when Jesus was twelve and thirty, as he began his public ministry, Luke offers another summary statement. "And Jesus **kept increasing in wisdom** and stature, and in favor with God and men" (Luke 2:52 NASB, emphasis added). As a man, Jesus grew up physically and socially. But as a man, Jesus also grew in wisdom and the fear of God. If you are struggling to figure out how God the Son could *grow* in the fear of *God*, that's OK. The Bible affirms Jesus' full deity and his full humanity. While we do not have to understand it all, it is certainly true. Luke, speaking of Jesus' humanity, clearly says the first thirty years of Jesus' life was marked by a developing wisdom. As he learned the truths of God, Jesus continued skillfully to apply them within the ever-changing details of his world. And he did so, perfectly.

Evidence 3: **The Direct Comparison with Solomon**

I love a good contest. It's great to compete and seek to improve your skills in a game or a sporting event. But it's also great to watch the finest athletes go head-to-head in a competition to determine which one of them is "the best of the best." In the contest to determine the wisest of the wise the two all-time finalists would be Jesus and Solomon. Israel's wisest king in the Old Testament was given a supernatural endowment of wisdom directly from God. He feared no competitors because God had made him the wisest man in history. As a sinful creature, however, Solomon had many years of failing to live out what he knew to be wise.[2] I believe that in the end, however, Ecclesiastes is Solomon's book of wise confessions from his experienced life. It is like he says, "I tried it all, and the real secret to a successful life is to fear God and keep his commandments" (see Ecclesiastes 12:13–14).

Jesus, of course, never sinned once. He always feared God, and he always kept God's commandments. While Solomon was a recipient of great wisdom, it is fair to say that Jesus was the giver of that wisdom. Jesus completely eclipsed Solomon in both understanding God and his ways, and living out that understanding.

One of the proofs of the wonderful wisdom of Solomon is the visit of the Queen of Sheba recorded in 1 Kings 10. Solomon's famous wisdom was so well known that leaders from other nations traveled at great personal expense to honor him with gifts and to hear his splendid sayings. After the Queen's thorough tests and evaluation of all that she had heard and seen, she was dizzy with amazement. She declares:

> "The report was true that I heard in my own land of your words and of your wisdom, but I did not believe the reports until I came and my own eyes had seen it. And behold, the half was not told me. Your

wisdom and prosperity surpass the report that I heard. Happy are your men! Happy are your servants, who continually stand before you and hear your wisdom! Blessed be the LORD your God, who has delighted in you and set you on the throne of Israel! Because the LORD loved Israel forever, he has made you king, that you may execute justice and righteousness." Then she gave the king 120 talents of gold, and a very great quantity of spices and precious stones. Never again came such an abundance of spices as these that the queen of Sheba gave to King Solomon.

(1 Kings 10:7–10)

Jesus once commented on the story of the Queen's visit to Solomon. He said of his own sinful generation, "The queen of the South will rise up at the judgment with the men of this generation and condemn them, for she came from the ends of the earth to hear the wisdom of Solomon, and behold, something greater than Solomon is here" (Luke 11:31). In head-to-head competition, Jesus is *greater* than the wisest man in history.

Evidence 4: *Jesus Reveals the Wisdom of God*

Although the religious leaders of ancient Israel claimed to have the keys of wisdom and knowledge, Jesus actually said they kept everyone locked out because of their unbiblical rules and traditions (Luke 11:52). The true source of the wisdom of God is the Lord Jesus himself. Another evidence of his perfect wisdom is that he dispenses God's wisdom to others.

At that time Jesus declared, "I thank you, Father, Lord of heaven and earth, that you have *hidden these things from the wise and understanding* and revealed them to little children; yes, Father, for such was your gracious will. All things have been handed over to me by my Father, and no one knows the Son except the Father, and *no one knows the Father except the Son and anyone to whom the Son chooses to reveal him.* Come to me, all who labor and are heavy laden, and I will give you rest. Take my yoke upon you, and learn from me, for I am gentle and lowly in heart, and you will find rest for your souls. For my yoke is easy, and my burden is light."

(Matthew 11:25–30, emphasis added)

Those who were supposed to be wise and intelligent completely misunderstood Jesus and his work on the cross. Instead of humbly learning from the ultimate wise man, they stubbornly tried to silence him. On the other hand, the unlikely candidates for God's salvation, the poor and lowly—"infants" compared to the others—came to Jesus in droves. What made the difference? The Lord of Wisdom chose to dispense God's wisdom to them.

Born to be Wise

Some 700 years before air ever filled the lungs of the Wise Man from Bethlehem, the Word of God foretold that the Messiah to come would be a man rich in wisdom. Of the hundreds of Old Testament prophecies fulfilled in Jesus Christ, none predicted his wisdom as clearly as Isaiah 11:1–5. The promise of the Wise Messiah coming to rule follows on the heels of a chapter about God's judgment on Assyria. God used the wicked nation of Assyria to judge the Northern Kingdom of Israel. At the end of their usefulness, God said he would bring an axe against the mighty forest of Assyria—resulting in a mountainside of tree stumps.[3]

Against that background, chapter 11 moves from local deliverance to eternal deliverance by talking about the coming of Messiah.

> There shall come forth a shoot from the stump of Jesse,
> and a branch from his roots shall bear fruit.
> And the Spirit of the LORD shall rest upon him,
> the Spirit of wisdom and understanding,
> the Spirit of counsel and might,
> the Spirit of knowledge and the fear of the LORD.

And his delight shall be in the fear of the LORD.
He shall not judge by what his eyes see,
or decide disputes by what his ears hear,
but with righteousness he shall judge the poor,
and decide with equity for the meek of the earth;
and he shall strike the earth with the rod of his mouth,
and with the breath of his lips he shall kill the wicked.
Righteousness shall be the belt of his waist,
and faithfulness the belt of his loins.

(Isaiah 11:1–5)

While there is much these verses reveal about the Lord Jesus, let's zero in on what they say about his wise character. There are two facets of his character that demonstrate the wisdom of Jesus.

What will Messiah be on the Inside? *(Isaiah 11:1–3)*

Beginning with verse 2, Isaiah unfolds the sevenfold celebration of the Holy Spirit's work in the Messiah. Almost every one of the six attributes endowed to Jesus relate to the biblical wisdom we have been studying.

We have seen these impressive parallel terms before: wisdom, understanding, counsel, knowledge, and the fear of the Lord. All of these wisdom words are ascribed in full measure to the Lord Jesus Christ. Even the new term "might" relates to Messiah's wisdom. It is the power to execute his wise strategy. Along with the other attribute in this pair, "counsel," this term is used in a military context in Isaiah 36:5 which says, "Do you think that mere words are *strategy and power* for war? In whom do you now trust, that you have rebelled against me?" (emphasis added).

Not only will the Messiah be endowed with the spirit of the fear of the LORD, but also "his delight shall be in the fear of the LORD." The two-fold link between Jesus and the fear of God underscores its importance. All of the Lord's thinking and actions would be in total submission to the divine will of him who sent him.[4] No one ever feared God like Jesus did throughout his time on earth. Based upon the components of the fear of the Lord identified in the last chapter, consider the ways Jesus fulfills them. He always *realized who God was.* As God, he knew everything, but even as a man Jesus was the perfect student of the Scriptures, and was baffling the rabbis at twelve years of age in the Temple. Jesus also *realized where God was.* He lived every moment of every day in light of God's character and presence. Finally, he perfectly *realized what God required.* In his prayer in John 17, he could honestly say at the end of his life on earth, "I glorified you on earth, having accomplished the work that you gave me to do" (John 17:4). Jesus came to the earth to do the will of God.[5]

What will Messiah do on the Outside? (Isaiah 11:3–5)

The acid test of wisdom in the Old Testament was the way a ruler or judge would render verdicts, especially on behalf of the poor.[6] A person may have seemed wise, but until the keen pursuit of justice was observed, no one was convinced. "Will he or she be fair or play favorites?" was the question of the day. When the Bible said that God made Solomon wiser than anyone else, the very next story told in 1 Kings 3 is about the two prostitutes with the two babies, one dead and the other alive. The shrewd judgment of Solomon demonstrated his wisdom to Israel. "And all Israel heard of the judgment that the king had rendered, and they stood in awe of the king, because they perceived that the wisdom of God was in him to do justice" (1 Kings 3:28).

When Messiah came, he would not just have perfect wisdom hidden away in his brain; his perfect wisdom would show itself through just judgments. Isaiah describes Jesus as not merely judging by externals, but by precise wisdom and knowledge of the truth. He would be righteous, fair, and faithful for those who would need it the most. He would not be afraid to use the strongest means to carry out his justice. Any apparent absence of his wise reign now after his first coming will be more than made up for at Jesus' Second Coming. Final justice is certain for all because the Messiah, King Jesus is *perfectly wise*—and wisdom always shows itself in justice.

THE IMPORTANCE OF THE PERFECT WISDOM OF JESUS

Why does it matter so much that Jesus was the perfect example of wisdom? Because you and I are *fools*. As we continue the quest for wisdom for ourselves and for those we lead, it must not be apart from Christ. Whether we are wise men or fools counts towards our eternal destinies. Our only hope for a wisdom acceptable before God is the wise and merciful King Jesus.

He is the source of your life in Christ Jesus, whom God made our wisdom and our righteousness and sanctification and redemption. Therefore, as it is written, "Let the one who boasts, boast in the Lord" (1 Corinthians 1:30–31).

If you are in Christ Jesus by faith, then you are counted as wise before God. *Based solely upon that wisdom*, we must seek to know and live out God's Word in the world. As we move into the study of the different ways that wisdom in Christ is lived out, come back again and again to this foundation. Just because you are commanded to be wise and to control your temper, tongue, and sexuality doesn't mean you can do it by your own power, or up to God's perfect standards. The imperfections in our wisdom were dealt with on the cross of Jesus. And the basis for our efforts along with God's Spirit within us must flow from what happened on that same cross of Jesus. The wisdom of Jesus is no small matter. Every bit of our hope to make progress in skillful living is based on the foundation of Jesus' perfect wisdom.

Study Questions—CHAPTER 3

1. Regardless of a person's intelligence, God's wisdom is a heart filled with reverence for him that results in practical choices based on his Word. Briefly discuss the connection between wisdom and right behavior.

2. Describe the correlation between sinfulness and foolishness.

3. What are the eternal differences of a fool compared to one who is wise?

4. Based on 1 Corinthians 1:30, describe the wisdom of believers before and after the cross.

5. How does our position before God determine our wisdom?

6. Give at least four scripture references that describe the wisdom of Jesus.

7. According to Isaiah 11:1–3, list six attributes of Christ that relate to Biblical wisdom.

8. Describe the importance of Jesus as the perfect example of wisdom.

9. How does God view those who are in Christ Jesus by faith?

10. What hope does the believer have in his progress of skillful living?

GUT CHECK

No one has ever feared God like Jesus did throughout his time on earth.

    a. He always realized who God was.
    b. He realized where God was.
    c. He realized what God required.

• Based on Christ's example, how do you see yourself as one who fears God?

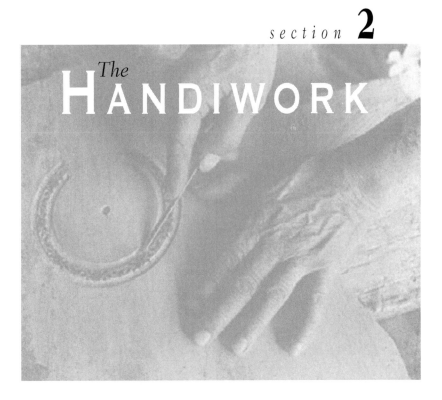

The
HANDIWORK

4

AS BUSY AS AN ANT

ONE DAY I CROSSED PATHS with a Christian man who owned a painting company. In our conversation he challenged me to learn to love hard work. He said a person who loves hard work would love all of life. How different this attitude is than the way typical guys think today. Some men gauge their entire life around their proximity to the weekend. If you ask them how they are, they grumble, "It's Monday." Later in the week they begin to perk up. "How's it going?" you ask. "Great," they reply, "Friday's only one day away." The implication is that the work week is bad, while weekends are good.

This anti-work attitude is completely unbiblical. While weekends are great, stay away from a weekend orientation. Avoid those kinds of expressions and do not think in such categories. Anti-work attitudes pollute your heart and negatively affect those around you. Instead of leading people in a wise lifestyle you could be dragging others down with you.

Becoming a man of craftsmanship means having your mindset about life shaped by God through the Bible. How does a God-fearer think about Monday? What does wisdom teach us about our attitude about working? Before we search the Proverbs, it is important to lay down some biblical foundations.

GOD MADE WORK

Discovering the original source of work surprises some people. Contrary to popular opinion, work itself was not a cosmic punishment inflicted upon humanity. God created work before the fall of humanity into sin. Everything before the fall was good.

> When no bush of the field was yet in the land and no small plant of the field had yet sprung up—for the LORD God had not caused it to rain on the land, and there was no man to work the ground, and a mist was going up from the land and was watering the whole face of the ground— then the LORD God formed the man of dust from the ground and breathed into his nostrils the breath of life, and the man became a living creature. And the LORD God planted a garden in Eden, in the east, and there he put the man whom he had formed. And out of the ground the LORD God made to spring up every tree that is pleasant to the sight and good for food. The tree of life was in the midst of the garden, and the tree of the knowledge of good and evil.
>
> The LORD God took the man and put him in the garden of Eden to work it and keep it.
>
> (Genesis 2:5–9, 15)

God designed even hard work for mankind's good. The difficulties of work today come not from a flaw in the design, but from the injection of sin. After Adam and Eve sinned in the garden, Adam's task grew painful. God, in response to Adam's disobedience, specifically added the sweat and toil factors to work that we still experience today.

And to Adam he said,
"Because you have listened to the voice of your wife
and have eaten of the tree
of which I commanded you,
'You shall not eat of it,'
cursed is the ground because of you;
in pain you shall eat of it all the days of your life;
thorns and thistles it shall bring forth for you;
and you shall eat the plants of the field.
By the sweat of your face
you shall eat bread,
till you return to the ground,
for out of it you were taken;
for you are dust,
and to dust you shall return."

(Genesis 3:17–19)

God's Work Ethic

What is sometimes called the Protestant Work Ethic sprang out of the English Puritans' diligent work habits. While the Puritans did not pursue riches and luxury, they often enjoyed prosperity because of their hard work. You could easily change the label, however, to God's Work Ethic, because faithful work habits are commanded in the Scriptures. The Apostle Paul had a strong exhortation to some within the Thessalonian church for their poor work habits. A group of them had stopped working because of their expectation of the Lord's soon return. "If Jesus is coming back, why bother working!" they thought. While they waited, apparently, they were leaning upon the generosity of the others in the church who were still working. Paul condemned that kind of thinking.

Now we command you, brothers, in the name of our Lord Jesus Christ,
that you keep away from any brother who is walking in idleness and not

59

in accord with the tradition that you received from us. For you yourselves know how you ought to imitate us, because we were not idle when we were with you, nor did we eat anyone's bread without paying for it, but with toil and labor we worked night and day, that we might not be a burden to any of you. It was not because we do not have that right, but to give you in ourselves an example to imitate. For even when we were with you, we would give you this command: If anyone is not willing to work, let him not eat. For we hear that some among you walk in idleness, not busy at work, but busybodies. Now such persons we command and encourage in the Lord Jesus Christ to do their work quietly and to earn their own living. As for you, brothers, do not grow weary in doing good. If anyone does not obey what we say in this letter, take note of that person, and have nothing to do with him, that he may be ashamed. Do not regard him as an enemy, but warn him as a brother.

(2 Thessalonians 3:6–15)

By Paul's example and clear command, he calls Christians to be faithful workers.

Men are motivated to hard labor for a variety of reasons. Some want more stuff. Some yearn to take exotic vacations. Craving recognition entices some guys to spend extra hours in the workplace. A man of wisdom, however, carefully works for a different reason. While providing for one's family, and even going on vacations are important reasons to work (see 1 Timothy 5:8), there is a more beautiful incentive behind hard work. The fear of the Lord inspires a disciplined work ethic even when no one else is around. Knowing that the Lord Jesus is watching challenges the wise person to labor faithfully. Colossians 3:23–24 challenged even those who worked as slaves with this mindset: "Whatever you do, work heartily, as for the Lord and not for men, knowing that from the Lord you will receive the inheritance as your reward. You are serving the Lord Christ."

This attitude does not lead to neglecting other responsibilities (like family or church) in pursuit of work, work, work. It does, however, radically affect what and how you fulfill your responsibilities in the workplace (whether it's a job, or in school). Throughout the Book of Proverbs diligent work is a characteristic of one who lives skillfully. Proverbs 6:6–11 offers two insights into the wisdom of being a diligent worker.

As Busy as an Ant?

The first insight comes in verses 6–8, where the wise person is compared to the ant.

> Go to the ant, O sluggard;
> consider her ways, and be wise.
> Without having any chief,
> officer, or ruler,
> she prepares her bread in summer
> and gathers her food in harvest.

If you think about it, it's pretty humbling to be taught wisdom from an ant. After all you are bigger, taller, and hopefully have a brain larger than an entire ant farm. You are being called upon to sit in your elementary school desk and learn from a teacher that is about a quarter of an inch long, weighs in at a fraction of an ounce, and is somewhat annoying.[1] Because wisdom is so valuable, however, stoop down, focus your eyes on these little guys and learn a couple of important lessons.

Be a Self-motivated Tireless Worker

Have you ever seen an ant take a break to rest? Can you imagine an ant offering an excuse for laziness? Do you think they ever sleep in, spend excess time around the water cooler, daydream about vacations, or take long lunch breaks? Ants provide an incredible example of faithful work. All the while, they perform their tasks with no boss breathing down their necks (see verse 7). Wouldn't it

61

be nice to trade your teenagers for a couple of ants for a Saturday of yard work?

Other Proverbs echo the ant's lesson of diligence.

A slack hand causes poverty,
but the hand of the diligent makes rich.
(Proverbs 10:4)

Whoever works his land will have plenty of bread,
but he who follows worthless pursuits lacks sense.
(Proverbs 12:11)

Whoever works his land will have plenty of bread,
but he who follows worthless pursuits will have plenty of poverty.
(Proverbs 28:19)

All of this land work, of course, would have been done without the aid of tractors or other modern farm equipment. Did you see the clear connections these proverbs made? The faithful worker will have an abundance of bread, while the one who chases after dreams is called a senseless person. Proverbs 28:19 is parallel to 12:11, only it replaces "lacks sense" with having "poverty in plenty." Which is more appealing, plenty of bread or plenty of poverty?

The issue is not a lack of energy. The word "follows" is an action word. Both the prudent person and the fool are striving for things. But the senseless man pursues *worthless* or *empty things*. The point is discrimination. Those who fear God have different priorities than those whose god is self. Idle fantasies, excessive devotion to hobbies, daydreaming, business speculations, and selfish pleasures all qualify as empty pursuits. Daydreaming can never substitute for diligence. How easy is it for a wife to follow a daydreamer? How motivated to serve the Lord are the kids of a wanderer? You must strive to faithfully fulfill the responsibilities God has given you.

Carefully Plan for the Future

The second lesson that the ant teaches is to work with an eye towards the future. Proverbs 6:8 says that ants prepare their foods in the summer and gather provision at the harvest. Another writer of inspired proverbs, Agur, agrees with Solomon's perspective of the wise example of the ants.

> Four things on earth are small,
> but they are exceedingly wise:
> the ants are a people not strong,
> yet they provide their food in the summer.
> (Proverbs 30:24–25)

There are several different species of ants in Israel that gather various grains in the summer in preparation for the winter. To walk in wisdom's way, we must do the same.

> He who gathers in summer is a prudent son,
> but he who sleeps in harvest is a son who brings shame.
> (Proverbs 10:5)

The lazy man doesn't eat and is an embarrassment to his family. The summer harvest began in May and June with barley and wheat. It ended in August and September with summer nuts and the last of the grapes. Working hard in the heat of the summer is not fun, but it is certainly wise. Poverty is not the *only* consequence of sleeping on the job. The Bible calls it shameful. Your reputation is at stake. Those who fail to work wisely gain the reputation of not knowing, not caring, and not contributing.[2] Part of the message of this verse is being alert to utilize opportunities *before they are gone.* Many fools become gung-ho workers right *after* their cupboards become empty in the winter. Yet they dreamed away the preparation time for the harvest.

The application is broadened in Proverbs 21:5, where planning ahead in linked with advancement.

> The plans of the diligent lead surely to abundance,
> but everyone who is hasty comes only to poverty.

Robert Alden comments, "More often than not . . . it's better to make plans than throw away time and money on something you haven't thought through."[3] Those who are diligent make plans and then work, not only hard, but skillfully to bring their plans to fruition. The wise worker strategizes to achieve maximum effort by thoughtful preparation and careful planning. Being wise is not just being the lumberjack who swings his ax the hardest and the most times in the day, but the one who takes time to sharpen his ax before felling the first tree. If you are hasty, quick, dirty, sloppy, and half-hearted in your work, you are heading to the same destination as the lazy daydreamer—poverty town.

Nap Time

Solomon continues the instruction about diligent working in Proverbs 6:9–11. He moves from the positive model of the hard working ant to the negative contrast of the lazy sluggard.

> How long will you lie there, O sluggard?
> When will you arise from your sleep?
> A little sleep, a little slumber,
> a little folding of the hands to rest,
> and poverty will come upon you like a robber,
> and want like an armed man.

Solomon almost sounds impatient as he repeats the questions, "How long will you lie down . . . ?" and "When will you arise from your sleep?" The illustration of the robber clinches his point. Poverty clings to a lazy man like a beggar that will not leave you alone until he has taken all that you have. Precious hours, important opportunities, and eventually years of productivity slip away like sand between your fingers. Why is this? A lack of initiative and enthusiasm in the person's work habits causes these miserable results.

Think about this. Does a sluggard ever set out to become one? When you ask a little boy, "What are you going to be when you grow up?" The boy usually answers: a fireman, a professional athlete, a police officer, or an astronaut—not a lazy bum. A little lazy selfishness makes little excuses here and there. "I'll just catch a quick nap." "How about a refreshing rest on a hot day?" "A little sleep, a little slumber, a little folding of the hands to rest" (verse 10). A lazy man's maxim is, "rest is better than work, and lying is better than sitting, and sleeping is better than waking, and death is better than life."[4] But soon the person actually begins to believe his excuses, and he develops habits of sluggishness. This self-indulgent lazy lifestyle ultimately will lead to his ruin.

Do not be tempted to excuse yourself if you do not qualify as an official sluggard. Are you a *hard* worker? Do you *plan* your days to get the most out of them for God's glory? Do you wake up and get to work a few minutes early? Are you thankful to God for designing work as part of his good plan? Do you remember who you are *ultimately* working for? Sure, some people are more self-motivated than others, but we are called to be motivated by the fear of God. Those walking in wisdom are God-motivated diligent workers.

Even as a young man it is crucial not to give in to your cravings to become a couch potato. Your job is to be a good student. Learn all you can in preparation for future service in God's kingdom. Some students come into school with the ability to easily get A's and B's. Others work very hard and only earn C's. While grades in and of themselves are not the determination of faithfulness, how hard you work is. Work hard to earn the best grades that you can. You will answer for what you do with the opportunities that God has put before you, and you will reap the rewards, or consequences, of how you spend your time as a student.

A godly attitude lived out in the classroom and the work place provides a stark contrast to others. While many non-Christians are good workers, many more are not. Some even work their hardest trying to get out of working hard. One hot summer I worked as a laborer for a general contractor. One day several of us had the task of raking rocks out of a newly cleared area of ground to prepare for fresh sod to be laid down. As I was raking, a co-worker called me out for working too fast. "Slow down!" he called out. "We get paid by the hour, not by the job." Others around you at work, at school, and at home notice your work habits. As Jesus said, "In the same way, let your light shine before others, so that they may see your good works and give glory to your Father who is in heaven" (Matthew 5:16). They'll ask about your diligence. Faithful work habits beautifully shine out against a dark world. Most importantly, however, God is watching, and his smile is your greatest reward.

Study Questions—CHAPTER 4

1. Based on the account in Genesis 2 and 3, contrast the work of man before and after the fall.
2. How should the fact that God is omnipresent affect our work ethic?
3. Regarding Proverbs 6:6–8, what two insights of being a diligent worker are offered?
4. Discuss the importance of discrimination as shown in Proverbs 28:19. What are the ramifications of a man's priorities?
5. What encouragement does Proverbs 21:5 offer those who plan ahead?
6. List some of the negative characteristics of the sluggard as illustrated in Proverbs 6:9–11.
7. What are the ramifications of being lazy?
8. How often do you plan your days to get the most out of them for God's glory?
9. What is the source of your motivation for hard work?
10. Describe the counsel that you would offer to those who are currently in school.

GUT CHECK:

"In the same way, let your light shine before others, so that they may see your good works and give glory to your Father who is in heaven" (Matthew 5:16).

- Based on your work ethic, what type of witness are you for the Lord?

5

SURROUNDED BY GOOD NOT EVIL

IMAGINE AN ART MUSEUM that has a collection of the finest pieces of art collected from around the world. Rooms are filled with breath-taking paintings, sculptures, and masterful displays. But suddenly, you smell the stench of a room filled with garbage. One entire section of the museum serves as a giant trash can. (I am not attempting to make any comments about modern art.) Your enjoyment of the art has now been replaced with an ugliness that you can taste. Just as a great museum could be ruined by its proximity to trash, a life filled with the skill of wisdom can also be desecrated by the things closest to it. You, your wife, and kids can become spiritually dull because you allow foolish people or things to rub up on you or them. Everyone becomes like that which surrounds them. The book of Proverbs, though, includes five ways to have wise surroundings.

Ways to Wise Surroundings 1: **Be Cautious Not Careless**

Once a king needed a new royal driver. He had his servants devise a test course through a winding mountain trail. At certain points on the course, the road traced the steep ledge of a tall mountain. The first driver swiftly steered the carriage to within three feet of the ledge. Not to be outdone, the second candidate wheeled the royal coach to within one foot of the great drop off. The third driver amazingly brought the carriage even closer to the edge. The final man, however, stayed as far from the ledge as possible. It was this man who got the job.

Being open-minded is supposedly the great virtue today. The only opinion that everyone in society agrees on is that there are *absolutely* no *absolute* rights and wrongs (never mind the glaring contradiction within that opinion). "We just need to be open-minded and tolerant," the world constantly tells us. The impressive observation about being open-minded, however, still stands: If you are too open-minded, your brain will fall out.

Proverbs 14:15–16 offer a wise observation:

> The simple believes everything,
> but the prudent gives thought to his steps.
> One who is wise is cautious and turns away from evil,
> but a fool is reckless and careless.

The naive are open to everything. Instead of being properly cautious of new and different ideas and input from unreliable sources, they believe everything. The naive guy is open-minded when it comes to good advice *and* bad advice, truth as well as lies, deception, manipulation, disappointment, and even danger.[1]

In contrast to the naive guy is the sensible man. This person is shrewd or experienced. He takes pains to verify what is before him. Using godly caution and care is wise. We all know when traveling in some foreign countries, wisdom requires asking questions about what food and drink to put in your mouth. What's called Montezuma's Revenge in Mexico is called the Sultan's Revenge in Turkey, and it has other cute names in other places. Being careless about what you let in your mouth can certainly be hazardous to your health. But being careless about what you let into your heart (and the hearts of those you are responsible for) can and will be hazardous to your soul.

John MacArthur is right when he says that the crying need of the Church is discernment.[2] Discernment is like the front door or gate that lets good things in, but keeps bad things out. Many homes in Florida are equipped with screened-in porches. The screen allows the sunshine in, but keeps the man-eating mosquitoes out. Discernment is the protective screen surrounding our hearts. Wisdom from the Bible, theology, experience, and advice from wise friends all build our discernment.

While the wise man in Proverbs 14:16 cautiously turns away from evil, the fool is *reckless* and *careless*. The pride of the fool leads him to reckless *self*-confidence. Even though danger is really present, he assumes he has things under control. Instead of trusting God and being careful, like a fattened bull strutting to the slaughter house, the fool carelessly walks right into risky situations.

Are you a careful man? While there is no virtue in paranoia, God says in order to be a skillful leader you must not be careless with what is coming into your heart. How dangerous do you believe sin is? Do the sources of advice you seek out matter? Does it make a difference how accurate the sermons are that you and your family listen to week by week? How much care do you take in making decisions affecting yourself and the others around you?

Ways to Wise Surroundings 2: **AVOID EVIL THINGS**

Though it may appear too obvious to say, living wisely involves actively avoiding evil things. Several Proverbs reinforce this plain truth.

> The prudent sees danger and hides himself,
> but the simple go on and suffer for it.
> (Proverbs 22:3)

When you see the sign that says DANGER: Bridge Out! (or Abyss Ahead!), don't you stop the car? How much more dangerous is sin than a bridge that is out of service? If you pass the warning sign and go off the bridge it could cost you your car, or even your life. But if you pass the sign that says, DANGER: Evil Ahead!, it could cost you your soul.

A related Proverb comes two verses later.

> Thorns and snares are in the way of the crooked;
> whoever guards his soul will keep far from them.
> (Proverbs 22:5)

If you walk along the crooked course, you will be snared. "The Bible teaches we should stay far away from the path of evil. If we don't even come near the place of evil we probably won't be tempted by it, and if we aren't tempted we probably won't fall."[3] This is so basic, yet so true. What are you tempted by? Can you take specific steps to avoid the temptation? If cookies are the temptation, hide the cookie jar, or get rid of it altogether. If watching too much or inappropriate TV is the problem, only watch it with someone else, or get rid of the TV altogether (it is really not as hard as it may seem). If you are tempted to stop at an Adult Book Store, drive home a different way. Our remaining sin urges us *to let ourselves become tempted.* This advice sounds a whole lot like Mr. Fool talking to us. Refuse to take his advice.

Fish love to eat worms, but the big fat fish are wise. They know something about sharp hooks cleverly concealed within the good looking worms. They have watched their friends and family naively gobble a passing pleasure to their own death. Your flesh loves pleasure, happiness, freedom from rules and responsibilities, money, self-indulgence and so on. Let's call each of these things worms. Wisdom stops and carefully reflects upon the big picture—eat worm, get eaten; avoid worm, and live. The foolish and naive (Fools-In-Training) dive headlong into passing pleasures and pay for it.

Ways to Wise Surroundings 3: **AVOID BAD COMPANY**

A third way to have wise surroundings is to avoid bad company. The book of Proverbs is *filled* with warning signs about the powerful and potentially deadly influence of a person's friends. While Christians ought to pursue casual friendships with unbelievers for the sake of influencing them towards the Lord, our closest friendships should be with the wisest people who will have us. The Bible specifically warns us of close association with at least six types of people.

Evil Men

Have you ever imagined being friends with a powerful mob boss (maybe after watching *The Godfather*)? Have you ever wanted to have a relationship with a seductive actress? Would you like to be close buddies with a rich business swindler? DO NOT DO IT! DO NOT EVEN WANT TO DO IT! Listen to God's wise words of warning.

73

> Be not envious of evil men, nor desire to be with them,
> for their hearts devise violence,
> and their lips talk of trouble.
>
>   (Proverbs 24:1– 2)

> Let not your heart envy sinners,
> but continue in the fear of the LORD all the day.
>   (Proverbs 23:17)

These people are sinful and foolish. And they will drag you straight into folly with them. "But their lifestyles look so fast and exciting. Maybe I could just drop into their lives for a little while and then slip back into the real world." Worms look so nice and juicy to foolish fish. Always remember the long view. Where will their sinful lifestyle take them in five years or ten years? It is possible you could have a little worldly fun for a while, but eventually your foolishness will likely result in imprisonment, an early death, and eternal destruction.

Gossips

Another party to avoid is gossips. They can not be trusted.

> Whoever goes about slandering reveals secrets;
> therefore do not associate with a simple babbler.
>   (Proverbs 20:19)

The verse warns against those who make friends by seductive flattery, and then turn and destroy their "friends" by violating their trust. A gossip is like a Venus Fly Trap, a plant which seduces flying bugs to come in close enough to capture them in order to eat them. If someone you know has a reputation of being a gossip, you are a fool to form a close friendship with him or her. The very least reason not to befriend such a person is that you are in danger of becoming the object of the gossip!

Angry People

A man of violence entices his neighbor
and leads him in a way that is not good.
(Proverbs 16:29)

Make no friendship with a man given to anger,
nor go with a wrathful man,
lest you learn his ways
and entangle yourself in a snare.
(Proverbs 22:24–25)

Solomon offers unmistakable words to the wise: Steer clear of angry men and women. We should do this because it is easier to learn sinfulness than righteousness. During flu season we all take extra care to avoid germs. We get flu shots, wash our hands more often, and load up on vitamins. Anger symptoms like impatience, a desire to control everything, and volcanic reactions to trials *are as contagious as the flu*. Skillful living involves level-headedness, self control, and patience. Those characterized by anger have none of the above. In Proverbs 22:25, Solomon's concern is that one would "learn his ways," that is, the path of his life, or his habitual lifestyle. The word translated "snare" refers to a striker bar, the latch that triggers the trap. If you adopt the foolish lifestyle of anger, you are doomed to step on the trap that will lead to your downfall. To avoid the downfall, avoid the trap; to avoid the trap, avoid an angry lifestyle; to avoid the lifestyle, avoid close friendships with angry people.

Gluttons

Gluttony is a lavish, frivolous lifestyle, where a guy drowns in undisciplined excess. They qualify as fools because of their selfishness. They spoil themselves instead of denying themselves. The

75

one who indulges himself is shameful. But an intimate friendship with someone who indulges himself is also shameful.

> The one who keeps the law is a son with understanding,
> but a companion of gluttons shames his father.
> (Proverbs 28:7)

Remember, the controlling assumption is that you become like those you spend the most time with.

> Be not among drunkards
> or among gluttonous eaters of meat,
> for the drunkard and the glutton will come to poverty,
> and slumber will clothe them with rags.
> (Proverbs 23:20–21)

Indulging in too much food or other excesses might not seem like a big deal. But gluttons are put in the same category as drunkards, sluggards, and fools. They are poor choices for friends. Both the act of associating with them, and the final results are a shame.[4]

Thieves

> The partner of a thief hates his own life;
> he hears the curse, but discloses nothing.
> (Proverbs 29:24)

Another group to keep away from is those who steal things from others. While certainly stealing violates the clear commands of God, even befriending a thief is foolish. This Proverb refers to the horrible result of such a relationship. You will find yourself hearing an oath or curse pronounced against one who refuses to tell the truth, the whole truth, and nothing but the truth with God's help. In other words, you will refuse to reveal the truth about your burglar buddy, even while under oath in a courtroom! What a great influence your new friend Mr. Sticky Fingers has been. Leviticus 5:1 says that the one who refuses to testify before the authorities is just as guilty as the one who committed the crime.

Sexually Immoral People

Some of the strongest warnings in the Bible are about avoiding the adulteress. Solomon tells his son that his wise words are given:

> To preserve you from the evil woman,
> from the smooth tongue of the adulteress.
> Do not desire her beauty in your heart,
> and do not let her capture you with her eyelashes;
> for the price of a prostitute is only a loaf of bread,
> but a married woman hunts down a precious life.
> Can a man carry fire next to his chest
> and his clothes not be burned?
> Or can one walk on hot coals
> and his feet not be scorched?
> So is he who goes in to his neighbor's wife;
> none who touches her will go unpunished.
> (Proverbs 6:24–29)

> Say to wisdom, "You are my sister,"
> and call insight your intimate friend,
> to keep you from the forbidden woman,
> from the adulteress with her smooth words.
> (Proverbs 7:4–5)

> And now, O sons, listen to me,
> and be attentive to the words of my mouth.
> Let not your heart turn aside to her ways;
> do not stray into her paths,
> for many a victim has she laid low,
> and all her slain are a mighty throng.
> Her house is the way to Sheol,
> going down to the chambers of death.
> (Proverbs 7:24–27)

77

Skillful living guards you from the fast but temporary pleasures of sexual immorality. Living in light of the real presence of Holy God is a protection from that sin which so easily entangles people (especially men). God warns against flattering words, seductive dress, and sensual expressions (the stuff of great looking worms). What is the outcome of a relationship with such a person? Being captured, burned, punished, and murdered all result from immorality (the stuff of very sharp hooks hidden inside of the worms). Wise men have no close friendships with immoral women.

Who are your friends? How would you characterize them? Which of you is the bigger influence in the relationship? Are your friends the kinds of people that you want to become? A careful selection of your closest friends is important because serious trouble surrounds bad company. Remember the character Pig Pen in the *Peanuts* comic strip? The cloud of dirt surrounding him affected everyone around him. The subtle influence of friends is usually indirect. Influence usually rubs off on us, more than it results from you consciously deciding to be like someone else. Keeping bad company virtually guarantees that you will get in trouble at some point, if only by association. Do not suppose you are above the wisdom of the Bible. The danger of bad company is not just a generalization. Never assume that *you* won't be touched by the selfish and foolish behavior of *your* friends. That line of thinking marks Fools-In-Training. The God of glory would not post so many serious warning signs if you were above the influence of your closest friends. Be wise enough to believe God, even when it goes against your feelings.[5]

Other potentially subtle influences can affect us in the same ways as close friendships. You may not have a foolish bosom buddy, but if you watch twenty hours of television per week, WFOOL-TV is having a definite effect (that would be KFOOL-TV for those west of the Mississippi River). In addition to TV, secular radio, magazines, novels, newspapers, the Internet, and movies can all speed us along the Fool's Highway. Many guys who would not dare to go naively to the street corner of the adulteress (Proverbs 7:7–8), gladly go to her website. Unfortunately, her website leads to the same hell as her house. Stay far away from both places.

Ways to Wise Surroundings 4: **SURROUND YOURSELF WITH WISE COMPANY**

The fourth way to have wise surroundings is the opposite of number three. Not only must you avoid bad company like the plague, but to become wise you must also spend time with those wiser than yourself. Proverbs 13:20 is one of my favorite ones in the book.

> Whoever walks with the wise becomes wise,
> but the companion of fools will suffer harm.

As you compare the two lines of the Proverb, what would you expect the outcome of being a companion of fools to be? Solomon leaps beyond the expected climax (becoming a fool) to the disaster that lies on the far side of your folly.[6] You will suffer the harm that your foolish friends receive. Why? Because by their influence you will become just like them.

Seek out godly heroes for friends. Spend as much time with them as you can. Just as foolish friends and influences *corrupt* us, godly wise friends *correct* us. They help us become wise as well. Notice the impact of the wise in Proverbs 11:30.

> The fruit of the righteous is a tree of life,
> and whoever captures souls is wise.

79

A wise man has a life-giving influence. He wins people by influencing them in wisdom's ways.

Ways to Wise Surroundings 5: **SURROUND YOURSELF WITH GOD'S WISDOM**

Since friends have such a profound influence, make the Bible your greatest friend (Proverbs 7:4). The Bible reveals God. The more we understand about him, the more we appreciate his majesty and glory. As we respond to that knowledge in godly fear (reverential awe), we advance along the Way of Wisdom (Proverbs 9:10). The Bible is filled with references to its own powerful identity.

> The law of the LORD is perfect,
> reviving the soul;
> the testimony of the LORD is sure,
> making wise the simple.
> (Psalm 19:7)

The testimony of the LORD is another way of describing the Bible. The Word of God is said to directly cause simple people to become wise.

> Confirm to your servant your promise,
> that you may be feared.
> (Psalm 119:38)

Remember that reverence for God is the foundation of living according to God's wisdom.

> Oh how I love your law!
> It is my meditation all the day.
> Your commandment makes me wiser than my enemies,
> for it is ever with me.

I have more understanding than all my teachers,
for your testimonies are my meditation.
I understand more than the aged,
for I keep your precepts.

(Psalm 119:97–100)

Paul's encouragement to Timothy for the coming difficult times was to make full use of the wise words of the Scriptures. He told Timothy, "From childhood you have been acquainted with the sacred writings, which are able to make you wise for salvation through faith in Christ Jesus. All Scripture is breathed out by God and profitable for teaching, for reproof, for correction, and for training in righteousness, that the man of God may be competent, equipped for every good work" (2 Timothy 3:15–17).

God's precious truth, which is found in his Word, teaches about his glorious person and work. This leads us to revere him, and to turn from self-centeredness towards God-centeredness. As you make life decisions from this heart attitude, you are beginning to make progress on wisdom's road.

Wisdom warns you to stay away from the dangerous edge. There is an abyss called foolishness into which you could easily plummet. Careless devotion to foolish things and foolish people leads you over the edge faster than we realize. The sin of a self-centered life is a serious matter. It leads to pain, death, and ultimately hell. If this is the path you are on, or if it is the path that your closest friends and influences are on, repent. Do a U-Turn in your heart, and come humbly to the Lord Jesus Christ for mercy. He truly delights in delivering people from their foolishness into the wisdom that leads to life.

Study Questions—CHAPTER 5

1. Contrast a person who is naïve to one who is wise in the following areas: advice from others, deception, danger.
2. What part does discernment play in guarding a man's heart?
3. Explain how Biblical wisdom, theology, and influence from wise friends builds our discernment.
4. Proverbs 22:3 gives what advice concerning things that are evil?
5. Describe the role of a Christian concerning friendships with unbelievers.
6. List six types of people that the Bible warns us about and why.
7. What advice does Proverbs 13:20 give concerning the company we keep?
8. Why should the Bible be your greatest friend?
9. How does Paul's advice to Timothy (2 Timothy 3:16–17) apply to us today?
10. Discuss the consequences resulting from the sin of a self-centered life.

GUT CHECK:

Do you consider sin to be dangerous?

- What amount of sin can you safely handle?
- How do you respond to sin in your life?

6

IF YOU CAN'T SAY SOMETHING WISE . . .

IF YOU'VE NEVER LIVED IN THE DESERT it is hard to appreciate the incredible impact of wild fires. The cameras don't do justice to the devastation of the wildfires in Southern California. Every winter, the rains cover the mountains with beautiful grass and wild flowers. The scorching sun, however, soon leaves the vegetation dry and ready kindling. The mountain waits to capture the first spark and then roars to life. Those living in places like Southern California can see the glow of the flames in the night and the ash raining down during the day. During a blaze they breathe in smoke all of the time. Acres and acres are charred each year by this devastating cycle. Sadly, these fires often close in on communities. When that happens the devastation can turn deadly. The Bible compares stray speech to stray sparks.

The words of our mouths can, if not careful, spark flames as deadly as the flames of a wildfire.

Care with one's words is another characteristic of the craftsman. If a person begins to live out the fear of the Lord (the beginning of wisdom—Proverbs 9:10), the results will include a transformation of the tongue. Not only will certain types of words drop out of his vocabulary, but the wise man will also replace them with good words delivered at the right time in the right manner. The Bible offers at least five lessons of skillful speech.

Speech Lesson 1: **WHEN YOU SHOULD NOT TALK**

The Danger of Speaking

The Bible tells us that often the wisest thing we can say is nothing. (That lesson may be enough for this chapter—let's close in prayer.) Many Proverbs echo the same message.

> When words are many, transgression is not lacking,
> but whoever restrains his lips is prudent.
> (Proverbs 10:19)

Some guys have the natural tendency to stream forth with words like a fire hydrant that is opened up wide. If you use many words, you are setting yourself up for sinning against others. When you stop to think about what you are saying, though, you have a much better chance of speaking with skill. Why do many words always lead to transgression? Because, as Jesus said, there is a direct pipeline between your heart and your mouth. Since you were born with a sinful heart, sinful speech is inevitable.

Without self-control acting as a mouth gate, a wild fool bursts out on the streets saying every unconsidered word that comes into his mind. Wide-open lips are like a waterfall flowing from a fallen heart. The fool's fountain of words is unrestrained and uncontrolled. His mouth leads him to financial, social, physical, and even spiritual ruin.

> Whoever guards his mouth preserves his life;
> he who opens wide his lips comes to ruin.
> (Proverbs 13:3)

> Death and life are in the power of the tongue,
> and those who love it will eat its fruits.
> (Proverbs 18:21)

> Whoever keeps his mouth and his tongue
> keeps himself out of trouble.
> (Proverbs 21:23)

David Hubbard put it well: "Eating words does not make for a pleasant diet. They can in fact, be poisonous—life-threatening in the guilt they generate in us and the hostile recriminations they spark against us."[1] Self-control with your tongue is an awesome duty.

Self-Controlled Speaking

The craftsman is growing in self-control. The control being developed in his heart will also help him lasso his tongue. There are many different occasions for a skillful tongue to show itself through its silence.

> The vexation of a fool is known at once,
> but the prudent ignores an insult.
> (Proverbs 12:16)

The point of this verse is not cover-up but control. The prudent person does not blast-off in public. During a time of conflict, he can absorb shame and restore his composure, which averts future conflict. Solomon notes the contrast as well. Sir Fool does not require much fuel before his mouth explodes. A foolish heart is impossible to conceal during a conflict.

Isn't it striking to see a person be slow to react? Wisdom leaves room for misunderstanding and allows the Holy Spirit to convict the other person of wrongs committed. If the other person knew everything there was to know about you in any given conflict, they would have far more legitimate ammunition to fire at you. This knowledge should keep you humble, open to correction, and patient with the other person.

> A prudent man conceals knowledge,
> but the heart of fools proclaims folly.
> (Proverbs 12:23.)

This verse does not refer to leaving out important facts like a man refusing to testify in court against a murderer. Concealing knowledge means waiting to be sure of what needs to be said. Instead of blurting out his first thoughts to the first person who approaches him, the craftsman makes sure he is speaking to someone who needs to know. He also takes care to see that the time is right to disclose what he knows.

> By the blessing of the upright a city is exalted,
> but by the mouth of the wicked it is overthrown.
> Whoever belittles his neighbor lacks sense,
> but a man of understanding remains silent.
> (Proverbs 11:12–13)

Nothing ruins a good strategy like having a spy reveal the plan to the enemy. This is true in warfare, business competition, sports, and many other realms. Between friends also, there is a time to keep your lips sealed. But sometimes a friend wrongly asks you to keep quiet about their sin, or a plan to harm themselves or someone else. At those times, you must break trust (but even then as discreetly as possible). As a rule, however, being surrounded by wise friends is very safe, because your most trusted secrets are safe from a neighborhood broadcast.

> Whoever covers an offense seeks love,
> but he who repeats a matter separates close friends.
> (Proverbs 17:9)

Love that forgives keeps quiet about a transgression. If someone sins against you, you must go to *them* with the matter (see Matthew 18:15; Luke 17:3). It is important not to point out his sin to *others* (if he refuses to repent, it may become necessary, however, to bring in others, see Matthew 18:15–17). If the person repents, asking for your forgiveness, you must forgive them. At that point all mouths become perfectly quiet. Loving forgiveness brings people together. Continuing to talk about matters, on the other hand, creates an iron wall, keeping people apart.

> Even a fool who keeps silent is considered wise;
> when he closes his lips, he is deemed intelligent.
> (Proverbs 17:28)

The saying goes, "It is better to keep quiet and be considered a fool than to open your mouth and remove all doubt." Many people give quiet people the benefit of the doubt. If you are not certain what to say in a given situation, remember Solomon's safe solution of silence. If you are currently a fool, but really begin to apply this counsel for quietness, you may not qualify as a fool for much longer.

The first lesson of wise speech is to know whether or not to talk at all. The key instruction that wisdom offers is self-controlled restraint. The foolish fellow's words will freely flow out of his heart as no protective gates or doors will hold them back. Prudent leaders, however, guard their hearts by keeping their words fewer but wiser.

Speech Lesson 2: **WHAT YOU SHOULD SAY**

Not only does God's book of wisdom help us restrain our words, but it also offers insight into the substance of sensible speech. As we make a second pass through the Proverbs, let's examine the contents of wise words.

> The lips of the wise spread knowledge;
> not so the hearts of fools.
> (Proverbs 15:7)

A wise man is not meant to be a walking and talking almanac flowing with trivia. The kind of knowledge that the prudent person spreads is the knowledge of God's will and ways. Like the farmer scattering seed, the whole community benefits when wise people are saying worthwhile things.

A fool does not necessarily lack in eloquence or intellect. Because of his anti-God attitude, however, he has neither the desire nor the means to spread knowledge. This is another clear warning about the connection between your character and your mouth. If you take care of your character, your leadership will take care of itself.[2]

> The tongue of the righteous is choice silver;
> the heart of the wicked is of little worth.
> The lips of the righteous feed many,
> but fools die for lack of sense.
> (Proverbs 10:20–21)

Good words are scarce, beautiful, and as valuable as silver and gold. The feeding in verse 21 refers to either literal productivity or feeding wisdom. The wise feed many people, while fools starve themselves and others. A wise person's heart is selfless and controlled, but the fool is self-absorbed. From the hearts of these two characters spring contrasting words and differing outcomes—one life and the other death.

> The mouth of the righteous brings forth wisdom,
> but the perverse tongue will be cut off.
> The lips of the righteous know what is acceptable,
> but the mouth of the wicked, what is perverse.
> (Proverbs 10:3–32)

The content of a righteous mouth is wisdom. A perverted mouth, on the other hand, is twisted, distorted, and ungodly. Like cancer it needs to be cut out. You must go to extreme measures to eliminate the effects of a twisted tongue. The acceptable speech of verse 32 implies it is acceptable to the Lord. A righteous heart produces speech that pleases God. In both of these verses, wisdom and foolishness are summarized in terms of personal behavior. The one who walks wisely and talks wisely is considered righteous. The one who flounders in folly uses perverted words and is called wicked.

Speech Lesson 3: **HOW YOU SHOULD TALK**

The third lesson wisdom teaches your tongue is the *godly manner* in which you should speak. It is not enough to use restraint. It is not enough to speak God's wisdom. The *way* you say the words you use is a critical component in wise communication as well.

> There is one whose rash words are like sword thrusts,
> but the tongue of the wise brings healing.
> (Proverbs 12:18)

The tongue can be a sword to stab *or* a bandage to soothe. We are quick to condemn those who kill with the sword, but what about those who murder with their mouths? Do you leave the people you lead bleeding and maimed, or medicated and bandaged? Pursuing God and the wisdom found in his Word will change the words of your lips. But wisdom will also change the way that you invest those words. The same needle can be used to pierce a person for harm or healing. What do you want to inject into the hearts of your hearers?

> A soft answer turns away wrath,
> but a harsh word stirs up anger.
> (Proverbs 15:1)

> A gentle tongue is a tree of life,
> but perverseness in it breaks the spirit.
> (Proverbs 15:4)

In a hotheaded dispute, a gentle answer sooths the hearers. It always takes two to have a fight. If one person tries to keep the flame burning, and the other continues to respond as a cool stream of water, the fire will be doused. On the other hand, if one person lights the candle of contention and the other person harshly adds gasoline, the fire burns out of control. The skill of self-control provides aid in gently responding to foolish attacks. The results of a gentle response are two-fold—wrath is turned away, and a tree of life shows up; that is, an uplifted, positive atmosphere is created.

> The wise of heart is called discerning,
> and sweetness of speech increases persuasiveness.
> Good sense is a fountain of life to him who has it,
> but the instruction of fools is folly.
> The heart of the wise makes his speech judicious
> and adds persuasiveness to his lips.

Gracious words are like a honeycomb,
sweetness to the soul and health to the body.
(Proverbs 16:21–24)

As the great theologian Mary Poppins said, "A spoon full of sugar helps the medicine go down." Lasting benefits of wise counsel are sometimes lost simply because of the manner in which the advice was given. Like medicine refused because it tastes so bad, some great counsel is refused because of the taste to the ears. The prudent person carefully considers what to say *and* the sweetest way to put it. What good are your words when no one will listen? Are your words more like honey or castor oil? The appeal of your advice will be directly proportional to the careful craftsmanship of your speech.

Speech Lesson 4: WHEN YOU SHOULD TALK

The fourth lesson of wise speech relates to timing. If you apply all of the other lessons of wise speech, but use poor timing, your wisdom will become foolish. As a doctor diagnoses a patient, many factors come together in producing a successful treatment. He or she carefully listens to the patient, asks probing questions to narrow the possible ailments, selects the precise medicine, as well as the most beneficial manner of administering it. But if the doctor errs on the timing of the medicine, everything could fail. If too much medicine is given too soon, or too little too late, the patient will continue to suffer. In the same way you must seek to skillfully say the right words *at the right time.* Achieving such a balance is beautiful.

A word fitly spoken
is like apples of gold in a setting of silver.
Like a gold ring or an ornament of gold
is a wise reprover to a listening ear.
(Proverbs 25:11–12)

> To make an apt answer is a joy to a man,
> and a word in season, how good it is!
> (Proverbs 15:23)

Knowing people are ready to hear a word, and then seizing the moment is a mark of wisdom. A good insight carefully thought through and carefully timed is the work of a craftsman. The expressions of the ornate golden apples in silver settings and gold jewelry reveal the attractiveness, quality, and value of precise timing. Joy and delight are the fruit of such efforts.

> The tongue of the wise commends knowledge,
> but the mouths of fools pour out folly.
> (Proverbs 15:2)

> The heart of the righteous ponders how to answer,
> but the mouth of the wicked pours out evil things.
> (Proverbs 15:28)

Skillfully using knowledge also requires a thoughtful response. The issue in these verses is not much or little talk, but considered or unconsidered talk. The righteous reflects on issues of timing, wording, setting, non-verbal communication, tone, truthfulness, and love. Any of these factors can affect the message. If your loving words are given with a grumpy expression, something is lost. Your wonderful message of compassionate concern will be lost if it's delivered during a commercial of the football game. Just as a beautiful diamond looks common when covered with mud, so a beautiful word loses luster when offered at the wrong time.

Speech Lesson 5: **WHAT YOU SHOULD SEE**

The final lesson of wise speech relates to *the results* of godly speech. When our words are wise God is pleased.

> Lying lips are an abomination to the LORD,
> but those who act faithfully are his delight.
> (Proverbs 12:22)

The Lord is the final judge of our lips. Only men who value his truth and righteousness will delight him. A heart that reveres God will produce words that please him. While wise words have wonderful earthly benefits, such as turning away wrath, ministering comfort, rescuing someone out of sin, and even bringing healing to a hurting soul, the ultimate blessing comes from heaven. God has carefully listened to every word from every mouth, for all of time in every place. And besides, he knows the heart attitudes and motives behind each of those words. As the Lord sifts through the sand pile of syllables, which words delight him? Words that are faithful and true are his delight.

The Proverbs of the New Testament might be the letter of James. Like Solomon, the Lord Jesus' half-brother gave strong warnings about our words.

> For we all stumble in many ways, and if anyone does not stumble in what he says, he is a perfect man, able also to bridle his whole body. If we put bits into the mouths of horses so that they obey us, we guide their whole bodies as well. Look at the ships also: though they are so large and are driven by strong winds, they are guided by a very small rudder wherever the will of the pilot directs. So also the tongue is a small member, yet it boasts of great things.

> How great a forest is set ablaze by such a small fire! And the tongue is a fire, a world of unrighteousness. The tongue is set among our members, staining the whole body, setting on fire the entire course of life, and set on fire by hell. For every kind of beast and bird, of reptile and sea creature, can be tamed and has been tamed by mankind, but no human being can tame the tongue. It is a restless evil, full of deadly poison.

> (James 3:2–8)

Even if you don't live in the desert, according to the Bible your mouth is still a wildfire threat. Our little tongues can do great damage. Words of gossip or slander, harsh words designed to cut, and even thoughtless comments can fuel a firestorm. Foolish tongues are like a dragon spewing out streams of fire. Sometimes the damages are deadly. The man seeking to live skillfully, however, controls his heart in reverence of the Lord. A controlled heart will produce a controlled tongue. A controlled tongue will strengthen those around it. Instead of a wildfire of destruction, wise words build up. They build people. They build homes. They build churches. They build communities. They build nations.

Study Questions—CHAPTER 6

1. Describe the vocabulary that characterizes a wise man's speech.
2. Based on Proverbs 10:19, why do many words always lead to transgression?
3. List four areas in which a fool will come to ruin due to unrestrained and uncontrolled speech.
4. Discuss the importance of "concealing knowledge" as described in Proverbs 12:23.
5. After studying Proverbs 15:7, contrast the spreading of knowledge by a wise man compared to that of a fool.
6. According to Proverbs 10:31–32, what are the outward manifestations of a wise man?
7. What is the significance of giving advice that is appealing?
8. List seven characteristics of righteous speech and why they are so important.
9. Give four examples of earthly benefits that are derived from wise words.
10. The ultimate blessing of wise words comes from heaven. Based on Proverbs 12:22 describe the words that delight the Lord.

GUT CHECK:

A controlled heart will produce a controlled tongue.

- Do you have specific areas of your speech that are not under control?
- If so, what does that tell you about your heart?
- Who controls your heart?

7

SKILLFUL SEX

GOD DESIGNED YOU TO HAVE A GREAT SEX LIFE. God made sex and he gave it to men and women to use liberally. He does not secretly hope you will hold back on the amount you enjoy. God's great concern for your sex life is *the focus of your sex*. As the master designer of sex, God knows how to get the maximum effectiveness out of it. God custom made sex for one man and one woman who are covenanted together in the union of marriage. Other than those specially gifted to serve the Lord as singles, God gave this physical relationship to husbands and wives to be enjoyed as one of his greatest gifts.

Some guys wrongly assume that living out wisdom in godly self-controlled obedience means life becomes boring. TV and the movies paint these pictures of passionate singles and married men living it up with a different woman in each new scene. These encounters are always steamy, romantic, and without regret. Everything looks and feels perfect every time. There are rarely, if ever, any crazy things like consequences—unwanted pregnancies, diseases, or divorces. This picture, though, is a LIE. It does not exist in real life.

Did you know the typical sexually active single doesn't have nearly the *quantity* or the *quality* of sex that the typical married couple has (Christian or non-Christian)? It's not even close! Did you know that the typical sexually active single is enduring a swarm of consequences and regrets? God's plan for sex is the best; maybe even better than you realize.

Does the art of living skillfully have applications in the bedroom? Does God really have wisdom for my sex life? Absolutely! Wise King Solomon wrote a wonderfully balanced section of Scripture that extols the beauty of pure love and warns of the dangers of sexual looseness. Immorality is such a strong temptation for so many men, God spends a good deal of space telling us how sex is supposed to happen. Proverbs 5–7 deals almost entirely with sex, but let's focus in on Proverbs 5:15–23.

Pursue Pleasure with your Wife

> Drink water from your own cistern,
> flowing water from your own well.
> Should your springs be scattered abroad,
> streams of water in the streets?
> Let them be for yourself alone,
> and not for strangers with you.
>   (Proverbs 5:15–17)

There are two parts of this passionate pursuit. The first part is *the singular devotion of the husband to his wife*. A cistern is a hewn-out basin that collected water, precious rain water or storage from a well. They were usually covered up to guard against evaporation from the sun. Because Israel is mostly a desert climate, cisterns and wells are extremely valuable. Water is your life, and here water stands for your wife.

Drinking deeply from this precious water speaks of indulging in passionate lovemaking.

Later Solomon continues the imagery by calling the woman a blessed fountain. In Song of Solomon, he describes his lover, "A garden locked is my sister, my bride, a spring locked, a fountain sealed . . . a garden fountain, a well of living water, and flowing streams from Lebanon" (Song of Solomon 4:12, 15).

The picture of waters flowing down the streets in Proverbs 5:16–17 seems to show that a wise man must never take his love and desires all over town. If you arrive at the Last Chance Gas Station on fumes, and are about to cross the Mojave Desert, what would you think if the bored employees were having gas wars with the last few gallons left in the station? You see them using the nozzles as guns to shoot the meager amount of gas all over the pavement. And you cringe because they are playing around with what should be precious. As precious as water is in Israel, so also should your sexual relationship be with your wife. It was not designed by God to be spread around with other women.

Sharing women is strictly forbidden by verse 17. God has given you *your* wife. She is not for another man. Neither are prostitutes or immoral women for you. They have been lots of other places. Remember, let your spring "be for yourself alone, and not for strangers with you."

> Let your fountain be blessed,
> and rejoice in the wife of your youth,
> a lovely deer, a graceful doe.
> Let her breasts fill you at all times with delight;
> be intoxicated always in her love.
> (Proverbs 5:18–19)

The second part of the pursuit of pleasure with your spouse is *the satisfying devotion of a husband to a wife.* God made wise sex to be the best sex on earth. In his master plan he literally commands you to soak yourself in pleasure by enjoying your wife physically. Don't just have a fountain in the desert—let it be a fountain blessed by God. Don't just have a wife, rejoice in and take pleasure in the wife of your youth. A skillful life includes lots of sexual joy and fulfillment. But every bit of that joy must be aimed at your wife.

> Enjoy life with the wife whom you love, all the days of your vain life that he has given you under the sun, because that is your portion in life and in your toil at which you toil under the sun.
>
> (Ecclesiastes 9:9)

The beauty and passion of God's design continues as the wife is compared to a lovely deer and a graceful doe. Her graceful, gentle movements and beautiful shape are not minimized. Instead, God *maximizes* these attributes and says, "Go for it!" As the buck affectionately chases his doe across the meadow, so the wise man chases his honey in the bedroom. (Doesn't God's wisdom seem so much more practical than the old guy sitting on the hill under the tree?)

The picture continues with becoming delighted with your wife's breasts and drunk on her love. Becoming drunk with alcohol is always a sin; but being drunk with love from your wife is God's perfectly wise plan. Far from being a necessary evil, or a quiet little extra, your physical relationship with your wife is an amazing gift from God. It is to be thoroughly enjoyed by both husbands and wives.

How can you cultivate this kind of relationship? The key to a great physical relationship is a high quality overall relationship. It begins with right thoughts about your wife. Such right thoughts will develop right attitudes. Loving actions will then flow from such a heart so full of wonderful thoughts and attitudes.

Answer these questions:

- Do you think of your wife as a special gift of God custom built just for you?

> House and wealth are inherited from fathers,
> but a prudent wife is from the LORD.
> (Proverbs 19:14)

- Do you pray for your wife? Do you pray about your wife? Do you pray with her? Are you thanking God for her virtues and interceding for her weaknesses?
- Do you dwell on her good qualities? Compliment them often?
- Do you treat your wife as you treat yourself? If you are one flesh with her, doesn't it make sense that if you hurt her, you are ultimately hurting yourself, but if you help her, you are the ultimate beneficiary? Paul says this in the section on spiritual leadership and submission in Ephesians.

> In the same way husbands should love their wives as their own bodies. He who loves his wife loves himself. For no one ever hated his own flesh, but nourishes and cherishes it, just as Christ does the church.
> (Ephesians 5:28–29)

- Are you cheerful around your wife or grumpy?
- Do you seek to make time just to be with her?
- When was the last time that you surprised her with a thoughtful note, or a special gift, or took a chore off of her list by doing it yourself? These sorts of things build a solid relationship.

- Do you give her affectionate hugs and kisses?
- Are you working to be a handsome husband for her?
- Have you kept the "courting" mindset? Or did you stop trying to win her affection once you got her down the aisle?
- Do you check-in with her during the day?

Sowing these kinds of loving heart attitudes and actions through-out the day will bear fruit in the bedroom. The point is not to manipulate your wife into better sex. Wise sex is never selfish sex. The best sex, on the other hand, always flows from the best relationship. Cultivating the overall love between you and your wife will always enhance your love-making.

The old saying, "Pretty is as pretty does," is pretty accurate. Godliness is attractive. You may not think your wife looks as good as other women do. My question to you is: What are you going to do about it? The loving leadership of the craftsman can even transform your wife's appearance. If all you do is tease her, insult her, or encourage her to work out more, she isn't going to change (at least not for the good). As a man pursuing wisdom, you must "step up" in your house. You must lovingly lead her in holiness. Help her with her sins. Pray for her heart. Encourage her to fear the Lord and walk in his ways. Hold her accountable to grow and change. You will notice a definite difference.

As you cultivate this kind of godly loving atmosphere in your home, there will be a direct improvement in your sex life. You will enjoy one another more in every way. As your day-to-day relation-ship unfolds in individual godliness, God's blessing will rest on your marriage bed. I don't think it is too strong to say the fear of God is the beginning of a great physical relationship.

As your physical relationship with your wife grows into what it should be, a tremendous side benefit is extra protection against sexual temptation. The old preacher Charles Bridges put it like this in 1846, "Tender, well-regulated, domestic affection is the best defense against the vagrant desires of unlawful passion."[1] Almost a hundred and sixty years later we might put it, "If you are enjoying steak and lobster at home, Happy Meals aren't nearly so attractive."[2]

BEWARE OF THE DESTRUCTION OF ADULTERY

Solomon moves from the glory of a wise sexual relationship between a husband and a wife to the ugliness of foolish sex outside of marriage. He begins with a loaded question and then gives three potent reasons not to commit adultery.

> Why should you be intoxicated, my son, with a forbidden woman and embrace the bosom of an adulteress?
>
> (Proverbs 5:20)

Just before this telling question, Solomon charged his son to become passionately delighted and intoxicated with the breasts of his wife. In direct contrast comes this charge to not dare become intoxicated with any other woman. The parallel language makes the warning crystal clear, but he enforces the command with three reasons to avoid adultery.

Reason to Avoid Adultery 1: **You Are Being Watched!**

> For a man's ways are before the eyes of the LORD, and he ponders all his paths.
>
> (Proverbs 5:21)

A great friend of all forbidden sex is secrecy. "No one sees us here in the dark. No one will know if we are in the next town. No one will be hurt if it is just me and my computer screen. We are completely safe." These, of course, are all lies passionately propagated by the world, the flesh, and the devil. As we have seen, wisdom's foundation is fearing God. Part of fearing God is the conscious awareness that he is watching you. You are always living in God's presence.

The point of this Proverb is not just that God sees in the dark, is it? God not only sees you, but he also cares about what you are up to, and he will judge you for it. The author of Hebrews says that God is a special avenger of sins against the marriage bed. "Let marriage be held in honor among all, and let the marriage bed be undefiled, for God will judge the sexually immoral and adulterous" (Hebrews 13:4). Paul says in 1 Corinthians 6:9–10 that adulterers go to hell. "Do you not know that the unrighteous will not inherit the kingdom of God? Do not be deceived: neither the sexually immoral, nor idolaters, nor adulterers, nor men who practice homosexuality, nor thieves, nor the greedy, nor drunkards, nor revilers, nor swindlers will inherit the kingdom of God."

Whether you are thinking about it in the heat of the moment or not, your Wedding Day promises are binding before God. He will hold you responsible if you throw them away even in just a night of foolishness. He knows all of your possible excuses, and none of them will work. He will judge foolish sinners. Being in the dark will not save you from his perfect night-vision. It is as if you broke into a Judge's house to commit a crime and got caught red-handed *by the Judge*. How well will you make out in his courtroom? Just because you haven't been struck down on the spot doesn't mean God didn't see and that you won't be judged for it. Your wife may not know yet, but be sure that God does.

The mercy of the Lord in forgiving even sexually immoral men is not a small thing. God can and will forgive even your stray thoughts in the grocery store check-out aisle. Because of the cross of Jesus, God will mercifully forgive sinners. If you haven't repented from a sex sin that God saw you commit, by all means put this book down and repent. But if you are coasting along the Fool's Highway counting on God's mercy to wash away all of your loose living, you should think again. While it is true that God forgives sinners, and that we will be repenting throughout our lives, it is also true that God doesn't leave us in the mud. He indwells us by the Holy Spirit and changes us. If your righteous standing before God doesn't motivate you to pursue holiness, you need to question whether you know the Lord at all. Even the most mature Christian should be awe-struck by the thought of the eyes of God watching his ways. That is an important reason never to commit adultery. There is also a second reason.

Reason to Avoid Adultery 2: **Immorality is a Trap!**

> The iniquities of the wicked ensnare him,
> and he is held fast in the cords of his sin.
> (Proverbs 5:22)

Have you ever been tied up with ropes? How much worse would it be to be wrapped tightly in cords and chains? The immoral man fancies himself to be living the good life. "I'm *free* from my rotten marriage. I'm *free* to sleep with anyone I please." Actually he's all tied up in sin. Wise Charles Bridges asked about the chains of immorality, "Does he think he can give them up when he pleases? Repetition forms the habit. The habit becomes a ruling principle."[3] The look can become lust. The lust can become a conversation or an e-mail. Those emotional connections can become physical connections. All the while chains of sin are wrapping your heart into a package. That package of chains, cords, and you, the "free guy," will be delivered to hell with a bow on top if you don't repent.

105

Reason to Avoid Adultery 3: **Immorality Will Kill You!**

> He dies for lack of discipline,
> and because of his great folly he is led astray.
> (Proverbs 5:23)

This potent warning recurs throughout the book of Proverbs. Yes, God made sex, and yes, God made you a sexual being. But if you use God's great gift outside of the focus of marriage, you will die. Of the adulteress, Solomon warns,

> For her house sinks down to death,
> and her paths to the departed.
> (Proverbs 2:18)

> Her feet go down to death;
> her steps follow the path to Sheol.
> (Proverbs 5:5)

> But he does not know that the dead are there,
> that her guests are in the depths of Sheol.
> (Proverbs 9:18)

Whether it is a premature death by a sexually transmitted disease or by an enraged husband, God's Word warns of the potentially deadly consequences of sexual sins. But even if God patiently let's you struggle on physically, the weight of guilt because of your compromise and failure is a walking death. And eternal judgment still looms on the horizon.

During America's War Against Terror, there has been much talk about terrorism within the borders of the United States. Soon after the attacks of September 11, 2001, a few people received deadly anthrax in their mail. The media mentioned specific Government officials being put on red alert. Do you wish you could get famous by becoming such a target of terrorism? How would you like your name all over the newspapers as the latest objective of Al Qaeda? Not at all! It would be utterly foolish to wish for such a thing. To be excited about fame at such a deadly cost is unthinkable. But do you realize that adultery is even more serious than anthrax? All anthrax can do is kill you physically. Adultery can send you to the grave but then also to hell under God's wrath.

Sex is a beautiful gift from a wise creator. God made it and wants his creatures to enjoy it to the fullest. His plan includes full indulgence in regular joyful relations within the boundaries of the covenant of marriage. Taking his good gift and using it in wrong ways is a sin. All sin has devastating consequences. Thankfully, God in his wisdom even made provision for sinful creatures through the gift of his Son, the Lord Jesus Christ. Even though sexually immoral men are under God's righteous judgment, Jesus willingly took that judgment for sinners on the cross. So while 1 Corinthians 6:9–10 says that adulterers are going to hell, the very next verse says, "And such *were some of you.*" Through Jesus, those that have failed to be sexually wise, can still know the beauty of sexual fidelity.

Study Questions—CHAPTER 7

1. God designed you to have a great sex life. Describe the importance of the *focus* of your sex.
2. Discuss the two parts of passionate pursuit that are found in Proverbs 5:15–19.
3. How does Solomon use the imagery of water when referring to a man's wife in Proverbs 5:15–17?
4. The key to a great physical relationship is a high-quality overall relationship. Describe the actions necessary to reach this type of relationship.
5. List at least five things that a wise man must lovingly do to help his wife grow in godliness.
6. Based on Proverbs 5:21–23, list three reasons why a wise man should not commit adultery.
7. Part of fearing God is the conscious awareness that he is watching you. Explain how being reminded of God's presence may affect a man's desire to commit sexual immorality.
8. Describe the potential dangers of allowing sin to form chains around your heart.
9. Immorality will kill you. Give at least three examples of deadly consequences that can arise as a result of sexual sins.
10. What is a fate worse than death that can result due to a man committing adultery?

GUT CHECK:

According to 1 Corinthians 6:9–10, adulterers are going to hell.

- Have you ever committed adultery?
- If not physically what about in your heart?
- What is the good news offered through Jesus Christ for those who have not been sexually wise?

8

HUMBLY RECEIVES CORRECTION AND INSTRUCTION

BUSINESSMEN SPEND GREAT AMOUNTS OF MONEY hiring effi-
ciency experts to suggest ways their companies can improve
productivity. Coaches constantly look for ways to fine-tune
their players for peak performance. Even artists benefit from
critics and teachers who suggest ways to perfect their work.
Each of these examples involves people and companies gaining an advantage through the input of outsiders. But in order
to be helpful, each of the outsiders must begin by discovering
and pointing out flaws in the ones being evaluated.

These people being helped have to welcome criticism,
sometimes even paying big bucks to receive it. If the advice is
good and they listen carefully to it, though, they can benefit

greatly through it. The same can be said of you and me, and we usually don't even have to pay for it.

How well do you receive personal criticism? Do you invite it and welcome it, knowing its outstanding potential for profit? Or do you hate it, getting defensive upon the first indications of its presence? Do you end up loathing the person who tries to reprove you? The way you receive criticism is a benchmark of your progress toward craftsmanship.

Dawson Trotman, founder of The Navigators, had a tremendous personal discipline. Whenever someone would criticize him, he would take it before the Lord in prayer. He laid each one of the points before God, asking him to show him the kernels of truth. I have heard John MacArthur suggest that you should be very gracious when being criticized, realizing that if the critic knew all the evil that was in your heart, he would have many more legitimate things to point out.

In striving to grow as craftsmen, we have been examining the character of wisdom. A person walking through life skillfully will be a diligent worker, surrounding himself with good things, and will take care with his words. Another beautiful and rare quality that flows out of a heart that fears God is a humility that is willing to receive criticism and instruction. While this quality violates the voice of the remaining sin within us, the Proverbs leave *no doubt* about its certain connection to wisdom. Consider first the relationship between humility and wisdom.

BEWARE OF PRIDE

> When pride comes, then comes disgrace,
> but with the humble is wisdom.
>
> (Proverbs 11:2)

Pride is the root of all self-love. If cultivated, this root soon grows up into a plant. Finally, it forms a tree of stubbornness that demands everything be its own way. Pride assumes it knows everything there is to know. The king of Egypt that held Israel captive was a classic example. As the Levites praised God for his wonderful works of old, they remembered the arrogance of Pharaoh and the Egyptians.

> "And you saw the affliction of our fathers in Egypt and heard their cry at the Red Sea, and performed signs and wonders against Pharaoh and all his servants and all the people of his land, for you knew that they acted arrogantly against our fathers. And you made a name for yourself, as it is to this day.
> (Nehemiah 9:9–10)

If you are cultivating a pride tree, the Bible says that God will turn your tree into dishonor. If you pump yourself up, God will bring you down. God accepts no rivals.

> One's pride will bring him low,
> but he who is lowly in spirit will obtain honor.
> (Proverbs 29:23)

There are severe limits to your strength and your knowledge. You do not know God's Word as exhaustively or experientially as you should. You are not adequate in your experience of life. Do you *readily* acknowledge these things? Do you ask for and receive help, input, comfort, and support from the Lord and from godly teachers and friends?

Arrogant insubordination never allows you to make progress in wisdom. Being stubborn in your opinions, unwilling to ask questions, and unwilling to ask for help are all marks of foolish pride. *God's wisdom is free and available, but sometimes it is painfully humbling to receive.* Because wisdom is worth so much, you must strive to go across the grain of your sinfulness and humbly receive wisdom's hard words. Moving from the general connections of humility and wisdom, we can now survey the specific ties between wisdom and receiving reproof.

KISS YOUR CRITICS

Growing in Wisdom

> Whoever corrects a scoffer gets himself abuse,
> and he who reproves a wicked man incurs injury.
> Do not reprove a scoffer, or he will hate you;
> reprove a wise man, and he will love you.
> Give instruction to a wise man, and he will be still wiser;
> teach a righteous man, and he will increase in learning.
> (Proverbs 9:7–9)

This passage calls for a careful (though potentially painful) inspection. These verses are about various reactions to those who give correction. The outcome of the very same correction depends on the heart of the hearer. The first hearer mentioned is a wicked man also called a scoffer. A scoffer is a fool in the final stages of his folly. David Hubbard calls him "a cynic par excellence." Hubbard continues by saying, "He scorns all good advice, probing for loopholes, jeering the motives of the teachers, and mocking the naiveté of those who try to do things right."[1] The courageous confrontation of such a person is rewarded with . . . dishonor and abuse. He not only returns insults for the efforts, but he also hates the one daring to challenge him. The scoffer is so far down the road to foolishness, he has a zero-tolerance policy for wise correction. Sometimes you meet a fool driving poorly on the road, perhaps endangering himself and others around him. If you try to offer the honk of reproof, at best it results only in scorn and retaliation.

The second hearer mentioned in these verses is the wise man (also called the righteous man). He realizes that he will never arrive at perfection in this lifetime. Though painful to hear, the man of prudence gives an ear to reproof, instruction, and teaching. He views the words spoken to him as an opportunity to grow in living skillfully. If you are to sharpen your skills in living life, you must learn to love your critics.

The Path of Life

> Whoever heeds instruction is on the path to life,
> but he who rejects reproof leads others astray.
> (Proverbs 10:17)

Do you want to walk on the path of God's blessings? Do you want to experience God's eternal life? If so, then *carefully listen to instruction*. Pride claims not to need teaching, but humility admits that there is much to learn. While *just* listening to instruction does not put you on the path of life, consistently listening can be an indicator that you are on the right path.

A skillful leader has to be able to both give and receive reproofs. The ability to receive reproof is a prerequisite to you becoming wise. It is not fun to be reproved—it's hard to hear about your sin; it's humiliating to admit you were wrong; it's tough to act on the instruction and correct your sinful behavior. *But* if you ignore such reproof, you *will* go astray. Where God's path turns right, you will begin to drift left. Where God's path leads to ultimate good, you will find yourself in misery.

The ability to give reproof, however, is also a vital part of influencing those around you to become wise. Godly wisdom is never an end for the craftsman. You have been entrusted with others to lead in the art of skillful living. This isn't always easy. Many people foolishly refuse to admit they are wrong. To effectively confront

113

them, you may have to do some homework. Search God's Word and make a list of the Scriptures that show them their sin. It will require prayer. Your goal must always be to help the person come back to the right road. Godly leadership requires humility to receive reproof and grace to give it.

Loving Discipline

> Whoever loves discipline loves knowledge,
> but he who hates reproof is stupid.
> (Proverbs 12:1)

How can a person *love* discipline? Only by looking beyond the discipline itself and thinking about the bigger picture. First, only a true friend cares enough to risk correcting another person. Second, this discipline will lead to greater Christlikeness (remember that *knowledge* in Proverbs is the knowledge of God and his ways). Third, behind this confrontation is a great and loving God who is at work in both of your lives.[2] Arming your mind with such thoughts ahead of time helps you to respond rightly in the midst of correction. Just as loving hard work requires a hope for the fruit of your labor, loving discipline requires the hope of Christian maturity.

The one who hates reproof is a stupid mule who will not turn no matter how the whip stings. How proud is the guy who will not listen to the correction of another? Do you really think you have *no* room to grow and change? Are you truly wise? Have you mastered the skill of living out the fear of the Lord? If you are remotely tempted to answer yes to any of these questions, beware of wrapping your donkey ears in low ceiling fans.

I Seem So Right

> The way of a fool is right in his own eyes,
> but a wise man listens to advice.
> (Proverbs 12:15)

This verse proves that the questions in the previous section are not over the top. The fool honestly assumes his lifestyle is correct and above the need for the helpful counsel of others. While to some, self-confidence is a great virtue, a fool's stubbornness arises from over-confidence in himself.

Listening to Your Parents

> A wise son hears his father's instruction,
> but a scoffer does not listen to rebuke.
> (Proverbs 13:1)

> A fool despises his father's instruction,
> but whoever heeds reproof is prudent.
> (Proverbs 15:5)

> Cease to hear instruction, my son,
> and you will stray from the words of knowledge.
> (Proverbs 19:27)

If you cannot stand discipline at home from your own father, you are well on your way to becoming an insufferable fool. Even unbelieving parents generally have the well-being of their children in mind as they discipline them. Nevertheless, even if they do not have their kid's best at heart, a loving heavenly Father sovereignly stands behind them. He is allowing all the parents say and do to occur. He can use even improper words and discipline to perfect Christlikeness in his children.[3]

If you are still living at home, pay extra close attention to these clear words of truth. If you think you are the exception to this rule, since you know far too much to accept the discipline of your parents, give God the benefit of the doubt. Sometimes you need to act on your parents' counsel by faith. It may seem wrong to you, but if it does not violate a clear passage of Scripture, follow it in spite of your feelings. Once, my parents wouldn't let me spend any more time with an older friend. At the time, I was crushed, but later their wisdom became apparent. They were exactly right. It is only the scoffer who is skeptical of the value of his parent's counsel, correction, and rebukes.

Nothing But Strife

> By insolence comes nothing but strife,
> but with those who take advice is wisdom.
> (Proverbs 13:10)

When you assume you know it all and that you are too big to be corrected, what is the outcome? Will you be surrounded by serenity? Will your neighbors, family members, and co-workers smile when they see you coming? Absolutely not! When you overvalue yourself and your opinions, you will create strife. To reverse the question, does everyone around you seem to be at odds with you? Are you always clashing swords with others? Do you ever wonder why no one seems to get along with you? If the answer to these questions is yes, your problem is pride.

The attractiveness of wisdom is displayed in contrast to such pride. A wise man always holds his own opinions with a measure of self-distrust. Therefore, he is always open to the counsel of others. The age, maturity, experience, and giftedness (or lack thereof) of the counselor does not hinder the wise-hearted from listening to the advice. How many times has the penetrating counsel of a child stunned you?

Crimes and Punishments

> Whoever despises the word brings destruction on himself,
> but he who reveres the commandment will be rewarded.
> (Proverbs 13:13)

Poverty and disgrace come to him who ignores instruction,
but whoever heeds reproof is honored.

(Proverbs 13:18)

There is severe discipline for him who forsakes the way;
whoever hates reproof will die.

(Proverbs 15:10)

As you strive for greater skillfulness the stakes become higher. Notice the huge rewards and severe punishments attached to humility and arrogance. Your lifespan is on the line. Are you surprised by the amount of instruction that the Bible has about the way you respond to reproof and discipline? But wait, there's more.

Really Listen

The ear that listens to life-giving reproof
will dwell among the wise.
Whoever ignores instruction despises himself,
but he who listens to reproof gains intelligence.
The fear of the LORD is instruction in wisdom,
and humility comes before honor.

(Proverbs 15:31–33)

To listen "to life-giving reproof" means more than standing still with a smirk on your face. Listening implies paying careful attention so the impact goes straight to your heart. A fool, however, rejects reproof even as it rolls off the reprover's lips. While he may think that he is hating the one who would dare to discipline him, who does the Bible say he really hates according to verse 32? Proverbs 15:33 goes on to vary the motto of the book of Proverbs, which is "the fear of the LORD is the beginning of knowledge/wisdom" (Proverbs 1:7; 9:10), to show that the fear of the Lord is *not just* the beginning of wisdom, but the entire pathway of wisdom. A reverential awe of God will provide instruction every step of the

117

way. The honor that follows the humble finds its contrast in the complete destruction that follows the proud.[4]

Rich Benefits

> A rebuke goes deeper into a man of understanding
> than a hundred blows into a fool.
>
> (Proverbs 17:10)

Even the wise need to be rebuked sometimes. Their response will prove their level of wisdom. The penetration of a rebuke is pictured as an arrow going deeply into the flesh of someone without armor. Those who drill for oil must dig deeply to find their reward. A rebuke to a wise man reaches down into his heart, and the rewards of repentance will gush forth. The wise are marked by a conscience sensitive to the input of others, while the heart of the fool is stiff and unresponsive (even to a hundred punches in the face).

Object Lessons

> Strike a scoffer, and the simple will learn prudence;
> reprove a man of understanding, and he will gain knowledge.
>
> (Proverbs 19:25)

> When a scoffer is punished, the simple becomes wise;
> when a wise man is instructed, he gains knowledge.
>
> (Proverbs 21:11)

Solomon points out that watching the punishment of a fool is helpful to the naive. Many people never even consider that their actions come with consequences. Can you imagine a criminal thinking, "Oh, I don't have anything to do for the next ten years, I think I'll commit armed robbery, and then go to prison!"? In these verses all three mindsets are included: the closed mind (the scoffer); the empty mind (the simple or Fool-In-Training)—who must be startled into attention; the open mind (the wise man)— who receives even painful reproof. The scoffer ends up being punished (physically and/or financially through a fine), the naive receives shrewdness and wisdom, and the wise man gains knowledge.

Persevering Ears

> Listen to advice and accept instruction,
> that you may gain wisdom in the future.
> (Proverbs 19:20)

Just as clay left out overnight needs more than a few drops of water to restore its softness and pliability, the more waters of wise input that pour into your heart, the more you will be molded into a wise person. The New King James Version of the Bible translates the second line of Proverbs 19:20 as, "That you may be wise in your latter days." If you accept counsel and discipline today, you will gain wisdom for the future. If you aren't sure that counsel and discipline are helping you, believe God's Word. Trusting the Lord now *will produce visible benefits in the future.*

Faithful Friends

> Better is open rebuke
> than hidden love.
> Faithful are the wounds of a friend;
> profuse are the kisses of an enemy.
> (Proverbs 27:5–6)

Once again, let's consider both sides of the craftsman's responsibility. If you are wisely receiving a rebuke, recognize that only a true friend loves you enough to risk your friendship to say the hard thing you need to hear. On the other hand, if you are ever to impact others toward godly wisdom, sometimes you will have to step up and be the faithful friend.

Weak love refuses to rebuke a friend who needs to hear it. That kind of love is not real love at all. If a doctor refused to cut out someone's cancer because he knew the procedure would cause the patient pain, he would be a terrible doctor. As cancer left alone can be deadly, so those with a sinful heart need true friends to help them in their time of need. True love inflicts a little pain, to avert massive pain later.

Weak friends offer many excuses. *"I don't think they will listen."* Are you sure of that? Are you forgetting that the sovereign God of the universe uses rebukes to accomplish his will in others (remember Balaam's donkey)? *"I don't want to hurt their feelings."* How much pain will they endure if their sinful tumor remains unchecked? *"They won't like me."* If they are wise, they will love you. If they are scoffers, you may be right, but it is worth the risk to be a faithful friend. The Bible says again and again that those who have the courage to confront you are your friends.

A Parent's Two Aids

> The rod and reproof give wisdom,
> but a child left to himself brings shame to his mother.
> (Proverbs 29:15)

Effective parenting includes being diligent in disciplining your children at home. The rod and reproof give wisdom. As we discover the close connection between humility and wisdom, let's pause to notice where this humble receptivity begins. Both the rod (physical spanking) and reproof (words of correction) need to be lovingly practiced when a parent's teaching is disregarded. We are born sinful.[5] Our cute little boys and girls come into the world as F.I.T.'s. They desperately need God's wisdom.

Sparing children the pain and hurt feelings of discipline is *not loving*.[6] It trains them to become bigger fools who reject reproof, discipline, and wisdom. All parents love to give their children things that they want, but it is critical to remember that *small children do not know what they need*. God entrusted us with those little ones for us to lead them to his truth. We must use loving discipline and instruction when that truth is disregarded.

FIGHT TO BECOME WISE

The **barriers** to listening to reproof are stupidity, cynicism, and pride. The **dangers** of not listening are that you will be destroyed without remedy (Proverbs 29:1), have your prayers be abominable to the Lord (Proverbs 28:9), face an early death, and spend eternity suffering in hell. The benefits of listening, though, are direction, rewards, wisdom, success, companionship, and ultimately eternal life.

When you sin and a faithful friend comes along, you are in for a fight. Not a fight against your friend, but a fight against your flesh. You must fight against your pride. Fight against being defensive, making excuses, and the temptation to strike back. (Oh, how tempting it can be to focus on *the way* in which your friend confronted you!) Fight also against the tempting emotions of hurt and self-pity.

Thank God for your faithful friend. Thank God for being behind the words of your friend. After all, God ultimately allowed them to discover your sin, put it in their heart to confront you, and coordinated the meeting. He also allowed you to hear every word they said. Even if your friend does not know all of the facts, or has mixed motives in coming to you, God knows all the facts, and he has perfect motives in sending your friend. Thank your friend as well for having the strong love and courage to seek you out (it is not overly common these days).

Like Dawson Trotman, lay the criticisms out before the Lord one by one, asking him to show you any sin that your friend may have missed. Confess your sins and repent heartily, thanking God for his grace given through the cross of Jesus. If there are any things that require restitution, take care of them quickly.

If you are building a fancy desk, you'd be a fool to glance at the plans once and then just do whatever feels right. In life, as well, it is easy to get off the right course. The world bombards us with foolishness. Even straying a step or two off the path of godly wisdom leads to serious trouble. We need faithful friends to challenge us and godly humility to carefully listen and do what they say.

God's beautiful plan of wisdom does not include independent individuals marching into heaven by their own intelligence and power. The Lord made us interdependent. To grow in wisdom and Christlikeness we need brothers and sisters in Christ. By the Lord's design, they are responsible for us and we are responsible for them. Though it is not easy to confront or be confronted, knowing the splendor of God's perfect plan makes participation a delight, not merely a duty.

Study Questions—CHAPTER 8

1. Why is it important to be gracious when being criticized?
2. According to Proverbs 29:23, what is God's response to unrepentant pride?
3. Discuss how the outcome of correction differs based on the heart of the scoffer and the wise man, as told in Proverbs 9:7–9.
4. When considering reproof, what two functions must a skillful leader perform?
5. When giving reproof, your goal must always be to help the person come back to the right road. What forms of preparation will help you to accomplish the goal as you confront the individual?
6. List three things that will serve as helpful reminders to love discipline.
7. What advice would you offer a person who is living at home in responding to their parent's discipline?
8. Explain how a wise man's response to rebuke determines his level of wisdom.
9. Review Proverbs 19:25 and 21:11. Identify the three mindsets that are portrayed in these verses. Describe the outcome of reproof for each.
10. The barriers to listening to reproof are stupidity, cynicism, and pride. According to Proverbs 28:9 and 29:1, give four dangers of not listening. Contrast the dangers of not listening with the benefits received from listening.

GUT CHECK:

To grow in wisdom and become more like Christ, we need faithful Christian brothers and sisters.

- Which of your friends have confronted you regarding your sin?
- To whom have you lovingly and prayerfully offered a rebuke?
- In both cases, was the experience a duty or a delight?

9

TAMING THE TEMPER

THE KING OF SELF-INDULGENCE

One of the poorest examples of self-control in the Bible was Saul, Israel's first king. Throughout his reign he flared with impatience and acted rashly. Saul's self-control was so small, it contributed to his loss of God's blessing, loss of his kingdom, loss of his mind, and eventually the loss of his life.

First Samuel 13:8–10 records Saul's impatience on the battlefield when Samuel delayed. "He waited seven days, the time appointed by Samuel. But Samuel did not come to Gilgal, and the people were scattering from him. So Saul said, 'Bring the burnt offering here to me, and the peace offerings.' And he offered the burnt offering. As soon as he had finished offering the burnt offering, behold, Samuel came. And Saul went out to meet him and greet him." God never permitted kings to perform the sacrifices before the battles; this was for the priests. Instead of trusting the Lord to bring Samuel, Saul looked at the people and panicked. He illegally took matters into his own hands and suffered for doing so.

During another battle King Saul's weak self-control displayed itself again. "And he took Agag the king of the Amalekites alive and devoted to destruction all the people with the edge of the sword. But Saul and the people spared Agag and the best of the sheep and of the oxen and of the fattened calves and the lambs, and all that was good, and would not utterly destroy them. All that was despised and worthless they devoted to destruction" (1 Samuel 15:8–9). Although God had commanded him to *completely* wipe out the Amalekites, Saul disobediently indulged in the spoils of the enemy and left their king alive.

As David grew in popularity among God's people, Saul reacted in cruel anger.

First Samuel 18:8–9 says, "And Saul was very angry, and this saying displeased him. He said, 'They have ascribed to David ten thousands, and to me they have ascribed thousands, and what more can he have but the kingdom?' And Saul eyed David from that day on."

In two distinct fits of rage Saul actually tried to pin David to the wall with his spear.

The next day a harmful spirit from God rushed upon Saul, and he raved within his house while David was playing the lyre, as he did day by day. Saul had his spear in his hand. And Saul hurled the spear, for he thought, "I will pin David to the wall." But David evaded him twice. Saul was afraid of David because the LORD was with him but had departed from Saul.

(1 Samuel 18:10–12)

And there was war again. And David went out and fought with the Philistines and struck them with a great blow, so that they fled before him. Then a harmful spirit from the Lord came upon Saul, as he sat in his house with his spear in his hand. And David was playing the lyre. And Saul sought to pin David to the wall with the spear, but he eluded Saul, so that he struck the spear into the wall. And David fled and escaped that night.

(1 Samuel 19:8–10)

When the king's son Jonathon dared to show kindness to David, Saul became ferociously angry. This time he took aim at his own son.

Then Saul's anger was kindled against Jonathan, and he said to him, "You son of a perverse, rebellious woman, do I not know that you have chosen the son of Jesse to your own shame, and to the shame of your mother's nakedness? For as long as the son of Jesse lives on the earth, neither you nor your kingdom shall be established. Therefore send and bring him to me, for he shall surely die." Then Jonathan answered Saul his father, "Why should he be put to death? What has he done?" But Saul hurled his spear at him to strike him. So Jonathan knew that his father was determined to put David to death. And Jonathan rose from the table in fierce anger and ate no food the second day of the month, for he was grieved for David, because his father had disgraced him.

(1 Samuel 20:30–34)

Later in 1 Samuel, King Saul's rage compelled him to hunt down God's servant David all over the wilderness of Israel. Though David mercifully spared Saul's life two different times, Saul had no controlling boundaries over his sinful heart. The foolish man, like Israel's first king, follows his emotional reactions wherever they take him.

THE KING OF SELF-CONTROL

There could be no better example of self-control than the Lord Jesus Christ. Certainly he is the personification of the skillful

127

life that wisdom teaches. *Not once* did Jesus lose his temper. He never became impatient and disobeyed his Father. He never came to the end of his fuse and lashed back against one of his tormenters. The Lord Jesus Christ perfectly obeyed God with complete self-control.

It would be easy to assume that perfect Jesus must not have had to suffer like some of us: I'd be pretty self-controlled too, if life went my way more. After all, did Jesus ever get stuck in downtown traffic? He never had to work with a boss like mine. His family get-togethers could not have been as tempting as ours. He never had a two-year old.

On the contrary, Jesus actually endured *more* suffering and abuse than anyone in history. Even though the specific temptations he endured were different in the details, he faced every kind of temptation you face. For example, during the time leading to the cross, consider the multiple warheads Jesus encountered. *The world* around him was attempting to draw him into sin. *Satan* was rabidly enticing him to react sinfully. His *earthly enemies* hurled abuse, physically spitting upon him, punching him, whipping him, and ultimately torturing him to death on the cross. Even *Jesus' followers* were wavering in unbelief and prayerlessness, and deserted him in his hour of need. Finally, on the cross *God himself* poured out wrath upon Jesus, not for his own sins, but for the sins of all people everywhere who would believe. While God the Father was not tempting Jesus, God's actions certainly intensified the weight upon Jesus' back.

While we sometimes react sinfully at insignificant things like a slow traffic signal, Jesus responded with perfect skill throughout his massive trials.

> For to this you have been called, because Christ also suffered for you, leaving you an example, so that you might follow in his steps. He committed no sin, neither was deceit found in his mouth. When

he was reviled, he did not revile in return; when he suffered, he did not threaten, but continued entrusting himself to him who judges justly. He himself bore our sins in his body on the tree, that we might die to sin and live to righteousness. By his wounds you have been healed.

(1 Peter 2:21–24)

Jesus was *never* sinfully angry. He did not strike back. Violent retaliation was not even an option for Jesus. He was not stewing on his rights. He wasn't hungry to send his attackers to hell. He simply kept entrusting himself to God and to his ultimate justice.

Wisdom is the art of skillful living. Like a craftsman, the wise person applies God's truth to life's decisions. Skillful living begins with a proper reverence for glorious and majestic God. Such a view of God generates godly humility and a desire to glorify God in self-controlled obedience. God himself is also producing that kind of obedience within his children through the Holy Spirit.[1] We have already seen the attractive fruit of self-control that wisdom bears in several areas. The wise man is a hard worker, careful with words, sexually pure, and he surrounds himself with people and things that are good and not evil. All of these characteristics require the self-control that God-fearing wisdom provides. Another desirable quality that skillful self-control generates relates to your temper.

HOW LONG IS YOUR FUSE?

Everybody and everything around us is flammable. The world system is anti-God.[2] The world is filled with sinful people. Our hearts are filled with volatile explosives and we continue to jump and bump as we interact with other flammable people. The question that Wisdom asks is, "How long is your fuse?" Do you have a short fuse so that the slightest spark ignites you to anger?

Or is your fuse long enough to give you time to extinguish the temptation with a godly response? While wisdom may not relate so much to your I.Q., it does relate to your P. Q., that is, your Patience Quotient. The Proverbs again guide us through wisdom's instruction.

> Whoever is slow to anger has great understanding,
> but he who has a hasty temper exalts folly.
> (Proverbs 14:29)

Solomon does not leave his students guessing about the relationship of wisdom and foolishness to patience and anger. The quick-tempered fool does not think about the issues that confront him. He reacts emotionally to pressures, criticisms, disagreements, and insults. Some metals are more flexible than others. When pressure is applied, the flexible metals, like the craftsman, will bend without breaking. When rigid metals are pressured, though, like the fool, they snap in half.[3] How do you respond when one of your children isn't paying attention and spills his drink all over the dinner table? What's in your heart as you are stuck behind the little old lost lady going twenty miles per hour under the speed limit? Your reactions to the small stuff reveal what's in your soul.

We've all seen college football fans go wild over their team. Great rivalries electrify cities and states. Where I live, when Georgia plays Georgia Tech, nobody hides his loyalties. In the same way the quick-tempered man publicly represents Team Fool. He reveals his folly like fans promote their teams. Having a short fuse and blowing up over an issue or blurting out angry words is like painting your face, waving a foam number one finger, and singing the Team Fool fight song. Proverbs 14:17 puts it as plainly as possible, "A man of quick temper acts foolishly."

SOME LIKE IT HOT

> A hot-tempered man stirs up strife,
> but he who is slow to anger quiets contention.
> (Proverbs 15:18)

> Scoffers set a city aflame,
> but the wise turn away wrath.
> (Proverbs 29:8)

A hot-tempered guy is easily irritated, itching to pick a fight, and has a short fuse. You do not even have to do anything wrong to be in a fight with such a man; if you are nearby, this guy will stir the pot of strife. Those who scoff at God set entire cities on fire. The one who is slow to anger, on the other hand, is hard to fight with. He is patient, long-fused, and calm. Instead of stirring up strife, he eases tensions. Instead of picking fights, he diffuses them, avoiding them altogether whenever possible.

Quarrels depend upon the people involved far more than the subject matter. It is possible to have excellent conversations about highly controversial issues. If a fool is part of the discussion, however, the smallest contention turns into an emotionally charged inferno. Do you throw kerosene on hot issues in your conversations? Or do you extinguish flames with gentle love? Self-controlled restraint leads to peace.

CONTROL OF OTHERS OR SELF?

> Whoever is slow to anger is better than the mighty,
> and he who rules his spirit than he who takes a city.
> (Proverbs 16:32)

Solomon uses an extreme comparison to show the value of self-control. The worth of personal character surpasses that of a mighty

131

conqueror. To put it in our terms, would you rather be known as a successful businessman who buys out smaller companies, or as a godly man who maintains patience when you are wronged? Is it more appealing to you to be one who rules others, or to be one who rules himself? Kipling said, "Keep your head when those around you are losing theirs and blaming it on you."[4]

COOL TALKER

> Whoever restrains his words has knowledge,
> and he who has a cool spirit is a man of understanding.
> (Proverbs 17:27)

Wise character is a multi-facetted diamond. The godly self-control used to keep yourself cool in conflicts certainly manifests itself in the words you choose to use. As we have seen, sometimes the wisest thing you can say is . . . nothing. The mouth speaks out of what fills the heart.[5] If you are foolishly indulging in sinful rage on the inside, guess what will escape to the outside? If, on the other hand, thoughts of God form the grid through which you analyze a situation, you will remain calm even in hot situations. Wise heart restraint allows for skillful mouth restraint.

Derek Kidner offers three reasons to praise such calm in the midst of life's storms. First, *remaining calm allows time for a fair hearing*. Proverbs 18:13 says:

> If one gives an answer before he hears,
> it is his folly and shame.

That lesson is amplified a few verses later.

> The one who states his case first seems right,
> until the other comes and examines him.
> (Proverbs 18:17)

Anger clouds our vision of right and wrong. Reacting in rage at the first news of an event is dangerously foolish. Not only is a response premature, an emotional reaction often pours fuel on the fire. Keeping a calm mind allows time for thinking through a response that honors the Lord. It also invites a more thorough investigation of both sides of the story. As the saying goes, "There are always two sides to every pancake, no matter how thin."

Second, *remaining calm allows tempers to cool.*

> A soft answer turns away wrath,
> but a harsh word stirs up anger.
> (Proverbs 15:1)

As we have seen, carefully reflecting on a reply is more effective than speaking the first thing that comes to mind.

Third, *remaining calm has a potent influence.*

> With patience a ruler may be persuaded,
> and a soft tongue will break a bone.
> (Proverbs 25:15)

Have you ever stopped to evaluate the effectiveness of a harsh angry speech? How has it made you feel when you have been at the open end of the cannon? What would those around you say about the lasting value of your anger in their lives? A calm word given at the right moment, on the other hand, mightily effects lasting change.

BEAUTIFUL FORGIVENESS

> Good sense makes one slow to anger,
> and it is his glory to overlook an offense.
> (Proverbs 19:11)

The Hebrew term translated glory is unusual. It refers to beauty. In Exodus 28:2, Aaron's ornate priestly garments were "for glory and beauty." The word *glory* in Exodus is the usual word, but the term *beauty* is the same word used in Proverbs 19:11. The term shows up again in Proverbs 4:9 speaking of wisdom.

> She will place on your head a graceful garland;
> she will bestow on you a beautiful crown.

When someone sins against you, others may think you look unassertive or wimpy because you grant forgiveness. But God says you look great—gloriously *beautiful*. Offering forgiveness to someone is one of the most God-like and lovely acts you can perform.

This week you may have received harsh criticism. You also may have had good reason to doubt the motives of the one who let you have it. How did you respond? Were you slow to anger or short-fused? Did you take offense and perhaps allow your feelings to become hurt? Or did you stay calm? After you heard their regrets, did you take the steps to overlook and cover their transgression?

THE PATHWAY FROM WISDOM TO SELF-CONTROL

The wise man is marked by a tamed temper. He controls his heart because of his reverence for God. Instead of indulging in anger and spewing deadly retaliation for his hurt, he offers a godly response in peace. An important consideration for those attracted to such a lifestyle is *how* wisdom produces this kind of self-control.

Wisdom begins with the fear of God. *A right view of God and his commandments* compels the wise man to obey. The thought of God's great majesty is an aid in keeping calm under fire. My right to become offended seems awfully small in light of such a big God. All of a sudden, *my glory and rights* are not the essence of life. A healthy reverential awe of the Holy One radically adjusts life's focus. While sinners will sin against you, adopting the humble mindset of the craftsman will keep your eyes on your great big God and not yourself.

The Bible teaches that "the anger of man does not produce the righteousness that God requires" (James 1:20). From the start, the one reverencing God knows his target—honoring God by not becoming angry. Whenever I react in impatience and irritation, I am violating the two greatest commandments, to love the Lord with all that is in me, and to love my neighbor the way that I love myself (Matthew 22:37–40). Other truths from the Scriptures also flank the person walking in wisdom, supporting his calm spirit.

God takes care of what our anger cannot accomplish. Why do we lash out in anger? A common reason is to intimidate and manipulate others to do what we want them to do. We also suppose that anger is an effective punishment against others who have offended us. The Bible, however, makes it clear that these matters are in God's hands.

> Repay no one evil for evil, but give thought to do what is honorable in the sight of all. If possible, so far as it depends on you, live peaceably with all. Beloved, never avenge yourselves, but leave it to the wrath of God, for it is written, *"Vengeance is mine, I will repay, says the Lord."* To the contrary, "if your enemy is hungry, feed him; if he is thirsty, give him something to drink; for by so doing you will heap burning coals on his head." *Do not be overcome by evil, but overcome evil with good.*
>
> (Romans 12:17–21, emphasis added)

Have nothing to do with foolish, ignorant controversies; you know that they breed quarrels. And the Lord's servant *must not be quarrelsome* but kind to everyone, able to teach, *patiently enduring evil,* correcting his opponents *with gentleness.* God may perhaps grant them repentance leading to a knowledge of the truth, and they may escape from the snare of the devil, after being captured by him to do his will.

(2 Timothy 2:23–26, emphasis added)

Another help in controlling your temper is *remembering the massive debt of offenses that you have owed to God.* Jesus told a story in Matthew 18:21–34 about a man who was mercifully forgiven an enormous debt, only to punish someone that owed him a comparably small debt. The powerful lesson of the parable is in the master's response to the report of the slave's actions. "Then his master summoned him and said to him, 'You wicked servant! I forgave you all that debt because you pleaded with me. And should not you have had mercy on your fellow servant, as I had mercy on you?'" (Matthew 18:32–33). Remembering the enormous amount of sin that God has forgiven you of, gives lots of grace towards forgiving others of their comparably smaller offences against you.

Wisdom is also *mindful of the long-view.* What will be the immediate consequences of my actions? If I react in anger, what will be accomplished? Won't my rage most likely add fuel to the fire? What are the potential long-term consequences of my angry actions? I could drive a wedge between this other person and myself so deeply that only God would be able to remove it. If, on the other hand, I choose a gentle response, what will happen? As a rule, a gentle response turns away wrath (Proverbs 15:1). Skillfully step back from the heat of the moment, and think about the potential effects of your actions and reactions. A moment of reflection about the future will help you respond wisely in the present.

What if King Jesus had reacted to his trials and temptations like King Saul had done? Instead of firing off spears, Jesus could have flung his opponents into hell. Instead of taking lashes and abuse, Jesus could have struck back. Instead of entrusting himself to God's care, Jesus could have taken matters into his own hands. What hope would there be for angry fools like us if Jesus had done so?

Christians are followers of the ultimate example of humble self-control. The Lord Jesus Christ demonstrated amazing love to those who hated him the most. It was not when we became charming men that he set his love upon us, but while we were his enemies.[6] Even now, how does he respond when you, who have so much more light than any time in your life, still rebel against his clear commandments? Such self-controlled love from him should inspire the same from us towards others.

Study Questions—CHAPTER 9

1. Compare the relationships of wisdom and foolishness to patience and anger as described by Solomon in Proverbs 14:29.

2. How do your reactions to the "small stuff" reflect what is in your heart?

3. Quarrels depend upon the people involved far more than the subject matter. Explain why it is difficult to fight with someone who is slow to anger.

4. List three benefits of staying calm as found in Proverbs 15:1, 18:17 and 25:15.

5. Describe what is meant by "beautiful forgiveness."

6. Wisdom begins with the fear of God. Why does a right view of God and his commandments compel the wise man to obey?

7. Based on Matthew 22:37–40, describe how becoming angry violates the two greatest commandments.

8. According to the narrative in Matthew 18:21–34, how does remembering the debt you owe God aid you in controlling your temper?

9. Why will contemplating the future help you to respond wisely in the present?

10. At what point in our relationship with Christ does he set his love upon us?

GUT CHECK:

There is no better example of self-control than the Lord Jesus Christ.

- Discuss the suffering and abuse that Christ endured on the cross.
- What is the correlation between you and Christ's suffering?
- Compare the things you must endure to those Christ endured.

10

SOURCES OF WISDOM

VOICES IN THE WORLD CALL FOR YOUR ATTENTION. They each claim to answer life's questions. Money says, "I will give you all you can imagine out of life." "I'm your real friend," says Pleasure. The Adulteress lurks in the shadows dangling keys she promises will unlock happiness. Mr. Evolution advises that since there is no God, let's live and let live. The TV Talk Show says, "All that matters is how you feel about yourself." Mr. News Guy states, "The world is bad, so why bother trying to be good." The School Guidance Counselor acts as though everyone makes up his own moral code. How can you and I sift through the variety of voices to hear the voice of truth? Where can we find true insight, understanding, and sound wisdom?

While a woodworker might read a book on building bookcases or take classes to become a craftsman, those seeking to skillfully live for Jesus must look to other sources. You know you need wisdom for yourself. You know you need it to pass on to those in your charge. The question is where do I find it? There are six springs gushing forth the wisdom of God.

Even though most of these sources have been indirectly touched upon throughout this book, it is crucial to give them careful consideration. Wisdom is essential. There are many ways to spend your time and energy. There are many voices around you claiming to help you onto the right path. You will never accidentally run a marathon. You will never just happen to become a doctor. In the same way, you will never accidentally become wise. Use these sources as points of accountability. How devoted are you to tapping into these springs of life? How much effort are you exerting to win wisdom's race?

Wisdom Source 1: **THE WORD OF GOD**

The book of Proverbs was written to impart wisdom (Proverbs 1:1–7). We have discovered many nuggets of truth from that source in our study. But the rest of God's Word is a gold mine of wisdom as well. Wisdom calls us to make an intense commitment to the Scriptures.

> My son, if you receive my words
> and treasure up my commandments with you,
> making your ear attentive to wisdom
> and inclining your heart to understanding;
> yes, if you call out for insight
> and raise your voice for understanding,
> if you seek it like silver
> and search for it as for hidden treasures,
> then you will understand the fear of the LORD
> and find the knowledge of God.
> For the LORD gives wisdom;
> from his mouth come knowledge and understanding.
> (Proverbs 2:1–6)

Attaining God's wisdom does not happen by merely pondering life under a tree. Wisdom requires action. Solomon urges his son to highly prize wisdom and do whatever it takes to get it. He calls his son to use his mind, ears, heart, loud prayers, and full intensity to search for wisdom like he has a treasure map with a big X marking the spot. Feel the passion of these words. Many people have experienced the desperation of searching for their child at a crowded event. A father cries out repeatedly, looking intensely, pushing people and obstacles out of the way, tuned in to only one goal, finding his child. Wisdom is not for the weak or the passive, but for the passionate and the devoted.

The *object* of Solomon's son's intense search for the source of wisdom is described in two ways. Proverbs 2:1 calls the source "my words" and "my commandments." In verse 6, Solomon notes that wisdom comes from God's mouth. Both of these messages are pointing the King's son to the Word of God. The Holy Spirit was superintending Solomon, so these words took form exactly as God desired and were included in the Bible. As you look at your Bible, imagine a large X on the cover. The Word of God is the hidden treasure of the wisdom of God. You must not expect God to just zap you one day. But if you are a faithful student of the Book, you will grow as a craftsman.

> The law of the LORD is perfect,
> reviving the soul;
> the testimony of the LORD is sure,
> **making wise the simple**.
>   (Psalm 19:7, emphasis added)

> Oh how I love your law!
> It is my meditation all the day.
> **Your commandment makes me wiser than my enemies**,
> for it is ever with me.
> **I have more understanding than all my teachers**,
> **for your testimonies are my meditation.**

I understand more than the aged,
for I keep your precepts.
(Psalm 119:97–100, emphasis added)

But as for you, continue in what you have learned and have firmly believed, knowing from whom you learned it and how from childhood you have been acquainted with the **sacred writings, which are able to make you wise for salvation** through faith in Christ Jesus. All Scripture is breathed out by God and profitable for teaching, for reproof, for correction, and for training in righteousness, that the man of God may be competent, equipped for every good work.
(2 Timothy 3:14–17, emphasis added)

Paul described to the young pastor Timothy his one primary tool for a life of ministry—the Scriptures. He said they *give wisdom* that leads to salvation through faith in Jesus. Then Paul declared that all of the Word of God is inspired and thus useful for four areas: teaching, reproof, correction, and training in righteousness. Each of these areas is an independent source of wisdom, and God's Word is profitable for them all.

The New Testament version of Proverbs might be the letter of James. For wisdom to take root, according to James, it must be applied. "But be doers of the word, and not hearers only, deceiving yourselves" (James 1:22). While growth in Bible knowledge is good, that knowledge must be lived out.

If the Bible is the primary source of precious wisdom, how diligently are you exhausting its riches? It is not enough to say that you love the Bible and believe the Bible. You are failing if you are merely a member of a church where the Bible is used. You must go on a personal treasure hunt. If the Lord Jesus appeared to you in a dream and said, "The source of my wisdom is found in Greenland," how fast would you try to get there? If he said becoming wise required walking on hot broken glass, I dare say, we would try to pull it off. Instead he said it is in his book.

Strive to go to the Bible every day. Read it; listen to it; ask it questions and search out its answers; think about it; memorize it. Wisdom comes when you begin to capture the point the authors wanted their original readers to get. Then bring that point to your neighborhood, and apply it to your life. Take the time, and exert the force necessary to dig out the Bible's treasure.

Wisdom Source 2: PARENTS

The second source of wisdom is the human means for your existence. Your parents, especially if they are godly, are one of the greatest sources on earth for wisdom. Even if your parents are not Christians, the Lord still allowed you to be raised by them, and he has many good lessons for you through them. Usually even the people with the hardest hearts still care for their children, and have many life experiences that can translate into wisdom.

Most of the book of Proverbs was written from the perspective of a father to a son. When you want a description of an excellent wife, however, you search out Proverbs 31. Interestingly, Proverbs 31 includes the words of a King Lemuel based upon the teachings of *his mother* (Proverbs 31:1). So the most thorough biblical picture of a godly woman results from a mom telling her son what to look for in a wife.

While you live at home, growth in wisdom includes carefully listening to and obeying the instructions of your father and mother. Once you launch out of the home, your parents should continue to be respected sources of counsel. It is foolish to ignore their words, disregard their instructions, and resist their discipline. Several examples from Proverbs clarify this point.

> Hear, O sons, a father's instruction,
> and be attentive, that you may gain insight,

for I give you good precepts;
do not forsake my teaching.
When I was a son with my father,
tender, the only one in the sight of my mother,
he taught me and said to me,
"Let your heart hold fast my words;
keep my commandments, and live.
Get wisdom; get insight;
do not forget, and do not turn away from the words of my mouth.
(Proverbs 4:1–5)

My son, keep your father's commandment,
and forsake not your mother's teaching.
(Proverbs 6:20)

Listen to your father who gave you life,
and do not despise your mother when she is old.
Buy truth, and do not sell it;
buy wisdom, instruction, and understanding.
The father of the righteous will greatly rejoice;
he who fathers a wise son will be glad in him.
Let your father and mother be glad;
let her who bore you rejoice.
My son, give me your heart,
and let your eyes observe my ways.
(Proverbs 23:22–26)

Ways Parents Impart Wisdom

A life skillfully lived is not an end but a means. It is a means of glorifying God, and a means of impacting others around you. The biggest beneficiaries of a wise man in the house are his wife and children. So as a son, you should learn wisdom from your parents, but as a father, you must teach wisdom to your children. What are the ways craftsmen pass godly skills to their children?

Word of God

The most obvious way a father can build wisdom into his children is by teaching them the Word of God. As Moses gave one of his final charges to the people of God as they were about to enter the Promised Land, he urged fathers to instruct their children in the Bible.

> And these words that I command you today shall be on your heart. You shall teach them diligently to your children, and shall talk of them when you sit in your house, and when you walk by the way, and when you lie down, and when you rise. You shall bind them as a sign on your hand, and they shall be as frontlets between your eyes. You shall write them on the doorposts of your house and on your gates.
>
> (Deuteronomy 6:6–9)

All of the time, in a variety of ways, Dads are to get God's Word into their children. The New Testament echoes this clear responsibility. In Ephesians 6:4, Paul instructs, "Fathers, do not provoke your children to anger, but bring them up in the discipline and instruction of the Lord." Certainly, God has given us our wives to help us in this task. Parents can teach their children God's wise words in many ways. They can read it in a simple version, read children's Bible stories, sing it, play games with it, memorize it together, teach catechisms, talk about applications, pray through it, take them to church, talk about what they learned in church, and make pictures of the stories. The possibilities are limited only by a Dad's imagination.

Stories

Another way wise family leaders can share wisdom with their children is through the voice of experience. Solomon included many illustrations about the rewards of wisdom and the consequences of foolishness. The entire book of Ecclesiastes seems to be Solomon in his older years describing the futility of his foolishness. He had acted foolishly and experienced its emptiness. He concluded by urging his hearers to devote themselves to God. He ended by saying, "The end of the matter; all has been heard. Fear God and keep his commandments, for this is the whole duty of man. For God will bring every deed into judgment, with every secret thing, whether good or evil" (Ecclesiastes 12:13–14).

Your stories do not have to be as tragic as Solomon's to be effective. But do tell your children of your failures. Teach them the things you learned. Tell them of your triumphs. Point them to the Lord as your help and strength. Most of us can remember our parents sitting down and sharing stories from when they were children. While kids won't remember the routine details of their childhood, those stories can be a heritage of wisdom. Some of the stories will live on long after the children reach adulthood. God designed the family to be like that. Be purposeful in sitting down with your son or daughter and illustrate God's wisdom through your story.

Of course, illustrating God's wisdom through stories should reach beyond your own experiences. Tell your children all kinds of stories. Read biographies of heroes of the faith. Use their accounts to instruct your family. Enjoy fictional tales as well. God seems to have given children an incredible appetite for stories. Satisfy their hunger and impart true knowledge at the same time.

Discipline

Though many in our world think they can improve upon God's timeless methods of instruction, the Bible is absolutely clear. God uses parents to impart wisdom to their children through carefully disciplining them when they disobey his Word. Spanking is a means of instruction. If a child is too young to understand commands, a swat can teach them their boundaries. For example, when an infant crawls over to a hot stove, a smack on the hand teaches them not to touch it, and spares them tremendous pain. If the child becomes enraged in their playpen, a swat instructs them to calm down. **All physical punishment must be done in a loving, controlled manner**. Many helpful resources are available to help parents in this area.[1] The key text in Proverbs is:

> The rod and reproof give wisdom,
> but a child left to himself brings shame to his mother.
> (Proverbs 29:15)

According to the Creator of the universe, children need both physical punishment and verbal instruction about what they did wrong. Many other Proverbs show the relationship of discipline and wisdom.

> Folly is bound up in the heart of a child,
> but the rod of discipline drives it far from him.
> (Proverbs 22:15)

> Do not withhold discipline from a child;
> if you strike him with a rod, he will not die.
> If you strike him with the rod,
> you will save his soul from Sheol.
> (Proverbs 23:13–14)

The rod is a means of removing foolishness from a child. Why is this instruction for the ages? How could it work in the twenty-first century? Fools live for themselves and never consider the consequences of their behavior. The rod helps our precious but foolish children realize there are consequences for sinful behavior. If all adults today had that one little lesson down, how different would our society be? According to Proverbs 23:14 above, some people would still be alive today (Sheol being the place of the dead) had they been disciplined.

Wisdom Source 3: WISE PEOPLE

Wisdom is caught as well as taught. Being around wise people and avoiding fools is the third source of God's wisdom. It is also one of the easiest ways of becoming wiser. You become like your friends, therefore, be extremely choosy about who your closest ones are.

> Whoever walks with the wise becomes wise,
> but the companion of fools will suffer harm.
> (Proverbs 13:20)

Fathers must not only guard their own friendships, but they also must be actively involved with the selection of their children's friends. Although it may seem like micro-management, few influences determine the direction of your sons and daughters more than who their friends are. Many young people will reject your guidance and try to manipulate you into giving in. Remember the big picture. Wisdom glistens with God's beauty, while foolishness destroys the soul. Isn't it worth upsetting your son or daughter now, to keep them on wisdom's path?

Wisdom Source 4: GODLY COUNSEL

One of the advantages of surrounding yourself with wise companions comes from the counsel they offer. This is the fourth source of wisdom. Those who know God and his Word are the best equipped to counsel you in times of crisis and decision. You will benefit far more from faithful friends who are skillfully applying God's wisdom to life's decisions than from short-sighted self-indulgent fools. Listen to the symphony of Proverbs.

> The way of a fool is right in his own eyes,
> but a wise man listens to advice.
> (Proverbs 12:15)

By insolence comes nothing but strife,
but with those who take advice is wisdom.
(Proverbs 13:10)

A wise man is full of strength,
and a man of knowledge enhances his might,
for by wise guidance you can wage your war,
and in abundance of counselors there is victory.
(Proverbs 24:5–6)

Oil and perfume make the heart glad,
and the sweetness of a friend comes from his earnest counsel.
(Proverbs 27:9)

Two pieces of advice will help you sort through wise counsel. First, make sure that you are not consulting those who will only tell you what they think you want to hear. Pour your heart out before a *faithful* friend, who knows God's Word, and has the courage to tell you the things you *need* to hear. Second, beware of consulting with too many sources. Decision-making is hard enough with a few godly opinions, too many opinions often make the wisest course more difficult to see.

The simple believes everything,
but the prudent gives thought to his steps.
(Proverbs 14:15)

Be humble enough to ask others for advice. Then think through the options biblically and prayerfully choose the wisest course.

Wisdom Source 5: INSTRUCTION/REPROOF/DISCIPLINE

We have already discovered that humbly receiving correction is a beautiful quality of the wise. Being attentive to words of instruction, reproof, and discipline is a way God advances his children along wisdom's path. Just a few verses will serve as a reminder.

> The ear that listens to life-giving reproof
> will dwell among the wise.
> Whoever ignores instruction despises himself,
> but he who listens to reproof gains intelligence.
> (Proverbs 15:31–32)

> Listen to advice and accept instruction,
> that you may gain wisdom in the future.
> (Proverbs 19:20)

Wisdom Source 6: GOD

The ultimate source of wisdom is the only wise God. He is behind all of the other springs of wisdom. In Proverbs 2, the charge to aggressively pursue wisdom is followed by the reality that God reveals it to the one who searches.

> For the LORD gives wisdom;
> from his mouth come knowledge and understanding;
> he stores up sound wisdom for the upright;
> he is a shield to those who walk in integrity,
> guarding the paths of justice
> and watching over the way of his saints.
> Then you will understand righteousness and justice
> and equity, every good path;
> for wisdom will come into your heart,
> and knowledge will be pleasant to your soul;
> (Proverbs 2:6–10)

The Holy Spirit must illuminate our minds for us to grasp God's wise truth.

First Corinthians 2:14–15 says, "The natural person does not accept the things of the Spirit of God, for they are folly to him, and he is not able to understand them because they are spiritually discerned. The spiritual person judges all things, but is himself to be judged by no one."

In a context specifically referring to right responses during trials, the Bible provides a striking promise for those who seek God for wisdom. "If any of you lacks wisdom, let him ask God, who gives generously to all without reproach, and it will be given him" (James 1:5). The author of God's book of wisdom, Solomon, received his immense wisdom directly from the Lord.[2]

God may answer your request for wisdom in different ways. For example, He might increase your appetite for the Bible. Your recall of the Scriptures may improve. God could help you make clearer connections between different portions of his truth. He might provide you with a commentary that opens up the meaning of a passage, or suggests helpful applications. You might find yourself surrounded by wiser friends. He may increase the boldness of your friends to offer you a necessary reproof. He might answer your prayer for wisdom through the godly counsel of your pastor or a mature member of your church. He might work through a theology book to help you reverence him more, changing your perspective on all of life. You could find yourself or others more noticeably experiencing the rewards and consequences of actions. God could, of course, act directly to make you wiser like he did with Solomon.

God has ten thousand ways to work wisdom into your heart. While he is always at work to perfect Christlikeness within his people, he has revealed these specific resources for us to pursue. He did not send us to Greenland, or to the hot glass pit, instead he designed other means. Are you willing to read and study his book, listen to your parents, spend time with the wise, seek out godly counsel, listen when you are reproved, and pray? These are the voices and influences that we must listen to in our world. Your diligence in pursuing God's wisdom will show how much you think it's worth. Ultimately, your efforts will show how much you think God is worth.

Study Questions—CHAPTER 10

1. List six sources of wisdom.

2. Wisdom is not for the weak or passive, but for the passionate and the devoted. Wisdom requires action. Identify the actions in Proverbs 2:1–6 that lead to wisdom.

3. Describe how each of the four areas mentioned in 2 Timothy 3:16 are a source of wisdom.

4. According to James 1:22, what must take place in order for wisdom to grow?

5. Describe your role both as a son and father in regards to learning and teaching wisdom.

6. Disciplining children involves both physical punishment as well as verbal instruction. Discuss the counsel given to parents in Proverbs 22:15; 23:13–14; and 29:15.

7. As a father, what are your responsibilities regarding your child's friends as well as your own?

8. One of the advantages of surrounding yourself with wise companions comes from the counsel they offer. What two pieces of advice will help you sort through wise counsel?

9. The ultimate source of wisdom is the only wise God. Discuss the instruction given in James 1:5.

10. Your diligence in pursuing God's wisdom will show how much you think it's worth. What does your diligence say about how much you think God is worth?

GUT CHECK:

The Holy Spirit must illuminate our minds for us to grasp God's wise truth.

- How much wisdom have you obtained on your own?
- What is your personal responsibility for gaining wisdom?
- Describe the steps you are willing to take to be a wise man.

ENDNOTES

Chapter 1 *The Meaning of Wisdom*

1. Richard Mayhue, *Practicing Proverbs* (Ross-shire: Christian Focus Publications, 2003), p. 33.

2. W. E. Vine, Merrill F. Unger, William White. *Vine's Complete Expository Dictionary of Old and New Testament Words* (Nashville: Thomas Nelson Publishers, 1985), p. 291.

3. David Hubbard, *Mastering the Old Testament, Volume 15A: Proverbs* (Dallas: Word, 1989), p. 45.

4. Derek Kidner, *The Proverbs, The Tyndale Old Testament Commentaries* (Downers Grove: Inter-Varsity Press, 1964), p. 36.

5. Ibid.

6. Hubbard, pp. 45–46.

7. Robert L. Alden, *Proverbs* (Grand Rapids: Baker Book House, 1983), p. 20.

8. Hubbard, p. 46.

9. Ibid.

10. Ibid.

11. Kidner, p. 37.

12. Hubbard, p. 46.

13. Ibid.

14. Kidner, p. 42.

15. Ibid.

16. Ibid., p. 39.

17. Ibid.

Chapter 2 *The Beginning of Wisdom*

1. Jerry Bridges, *The Joy of Fearing God* (Colorado Springs: WaterBrook Press, 1997), p.19.

2. Ibid.

3. See Genesis 3:8–10.

4. See 2 Corinthians 5:21.

5. Sinclair Ferguson, *Grow in Grace* (Edinburgh: Banner of Truth, 1989), p.32.

6. See Psalm 7:11, Psalm 139:7–12, and Revelation 20:11–15.

Chapter 3 *The End of Wisdom*

1. Graeme Goldsworthy's book *Gospel and Wisdom* is especially stimulating and helpful about the themes of wisdom in the flow of Biblical Theology and of Jesus as the fulfillment of wisdom. This work can now be found as part of *The Goldsworthy Trilogy* (Carlisle: Paternoster Press, 2000). The seeds that I drew from for parts of this chapter are found especially on pp. 347–351.

2. See especially 1 Kings 11.

3. See Isaiah 10:5; 15–19; 33–34.

4. H. C. Leupold, *Exposition of Isaiah* (Grand Rapids: Baker Book House, 1968), p.218.

5. See Hebrews 10:5–9.

6. Leupold, pp. 218–219.

Chapter 4 *As Busy as an Ant*

1. Hubbard, p. 99.

2. Ibid., p. 158.

3. Alden, p. 154.

4. Cited in George Lawson, *Commentary on Proverbs* (Grand Rapids: Kregel Publications, reprinted 1980, originally 1829), p.80.

Chapter 5 *Surrounded by Good not Evil*

1. Hubbard, p. 341.

2. See John MacArthur, *Reckless Faith: When the Church Loses Its Will to Discern* (Wheaton: Crossway Books), pp. xi–xvi.

3. Alden, p. 160.

4. Hubbard, p. 259.

5. Two longer passages in Proverbs reveal even more about the danger-ous influences of friendships—Proverbs 10–19 and 4:11–19.

6. Kidner, p. 104.

Chapter 6 *If You Can't Say Something Wise . . .*

1. Hubbard, p. 216.

2. Kidner, p.113.

Chapter 7 *Skillful Sex*

1. Charles Bridges, *Proverbs* (Edinburgh: Banner of Truth, first published 1846, Banner Reprint 1974, p. 58.

2. Read 1 Corinthians 7:1–5 to see the mutual responsibilities to one another of husbands and wives. Paul says that regular intimacy between married couples is a great help against sexual temptation.

3. Charles Bridges, p. 59.

Chapter 8 *Humbly Receives Correction and Reproof*

1. Hubbard, p. 282.

2. See Hebrews 12:7–11.

3. See Romans 8:28–30.

4. See Proverbs 16:18; 18:12.

5. See Psalm 51:5 and Jeremiah 7:9.

6. See Proverbs 13:24.

Chapter 9 *Tame Temper*

1. See Philippians 2:12–13 and Galatians 5:22–23.

2. See 1 John 2:15–17.

3. Alden, pp. 114–115.

4. Cited in Hubbard, p. 210.

5. See Matthew 12:34.

6. See Romans 5:6–10.

Chapter 10 *Sources of Wisdom*

1. One of the best is *Shepherding A Child's Heart* by Tedd Tripp, (Wap-wallopen: Shepherd Press, 1995).

2. See 1 Kings 3.